Senior
Secrets

Dixie Watterson

Publications International, Ltd.

Dixie Watterson writes about retirement, health care, and personal finance for seniors and corporate clients. She has taught college finance, offered financial advice as a stockbroker, and acted as a consultant to corporations. She enjoys the senior life and can be found on long walks with her dog, hanging out with friends and family, and occasionally traveling to a far-off spot.

ISBN-13: 978-1-4508-3810-8
ISBN-10: 1-4508-3810-3

Manufactured in USA.

8 7 6 5 4 3 2 1

Contents

The Best-Kept Secret

HAVE YOU NOTICED THAT there is no single day when you wake up and are officially a senior? The definition of "senior" can vary by 15 years or more! You can join AARP at age 50 (though you may not be ready then), get discounts at some fast-food restaurants at 55, buy cheaper movie tickets about the time you turn 62, and file for Medicare at 65.

Retirement age varies a great deal too. Much depends on the type of work you do, your health, and especially your financial circumstances. Some people retire at age 55, yet full retirement age for Social Security is 66 or 67, depending on the year you were born. Many seniors choose to ease into retirement if they can by working part time; of course, that also helps supplement their income. Then again, many people don't ever retire!

No matter what your plans, we've all seen that the economy can turn them upside down, forcing people out of work before they're ready or keeping them on the job longer because their retirement savings have dwindled. In *Senior Secrets* you'll find advice and ideas for making smart financial decisions, managing money, and getting the most from Social Security, no matter what your employment or living situation.

Senior Secrets has tips for saving money on almost every page. And there's a whole chapter devoted to the perks of getting older. The chapter is overflowing with ways to cut costs on everything from groceries to travel.

This book has everything you need to make the most of your senior years. You'll find little-known facts about health, nutrition, and exercise; tactics for negotiating the Medicare maze; and places to get good, low-cost medical care and equipment.

Your social connections are critical to your health and sense of well-being, so you'll find lots of ideas for strengthening your relationships and making new acquaintances. We also guide you in using technology to stay informed and socially active, as well as to pursue your interests. And you'll discover the abundance of opportunities to enjoy your leisure time at home and on the road.

Of all the senior secrets, there is a surprising one that you surely are discovering: Life can be very good for seniors! Senior status brings unexpected rewards. It can be a time marked by self-confidence and opportunities to grow.

In fact, research finds that seniors are among the happiest of the age groups. A recent study of people's attitudes at different stages of life revealed that seniors are more content than people in their twenties, thirties, and even forties.

So whatever your circumstances happen to be, relish the freedom that you've earned. The joys, wisdom, and equanimity that come with being a senior just might be the best-kept secret of all!

1 Secrets to Financial Peace of Mind

Just how much money will you need in retirement? If you are unsure, you are definitely not alone. Most Americans retire without knowing whether they will have enough money for their future needs, let alone wants. Less than half make a stab at figuring it out. And almost one-third *do not even want to know where they stand financially!*

Whether you've already retired or are approaching retirement, it's not too late to work out a financial plan—or to improve one that you already have.

Free, Quick, and Easy

Many people mistakenly believe they've stashed enough away for their golden years, while others worry needlessly. Find out where you are on the continuum by using one of these online calculators from reputable sources:

- www.aarp.org: Enter "retirement calculator" in the search box on the American Association of Retired Persons (AARP) website, and hit "enter" to get to AARP's calculator. AARP also offers a savings calculator.

- www.bankrate.com: Click on the retirement tab at the top of the home page, and it will take you to a page with a wealth of resources about retirement, including several calculators (one of which is a retirement income calculator).

■ www.fidelity.com: Fidelity has several different calculators on its website. Enter "retirement calculator" in its search box, and you'll be taken to a page with retirement tools and calculator, including a retirement income planner. You don't need to be a Fidelity customer to use its tools, but you will need to register by giving your name and e-mail address.

Smart Money Management

There are countless resources to help you get on top of your money situation. The first step, though, is to take the guess-work out of your decision-making. Create a budget if you don't already have one, or at least make a list of where cash comes from and where it goes. Then figure out your net worth.

Cash in and out

Where does it come from? Where does it go? Make a list of your sources of income. If you are still working, your job is likely your primary source. If you're not working, then like many seniors in the United States, Social Security may be the cornerstone of your income. Be sure to include income from other sources, such as a pension, investments, or rental property.

Then figure out your expenses. Look through your check-book, credit card statements, and bank statements, and make a list of what you find. Be sure to include mortgage or rent payments, insurance costs, and car expenses (gas, insurance, monthly car payments). Medical expenses, clothing,

food, phone, and other utilities also should be included—
everything you can separate out. Don't forget gifts. Do you
give money to anyone regularly or just an occasional birthday gift to a grandchild?

If you usually get cash from the bank or an ATM and don't
know how you spend it, start to keep track. Some budgeters
write down every penny, but the idea is to get started. You'll
get a snapshot of money that comes in and how you spend it.

Another important number is your net worth. It's what you
would have left over if you sold everything you own and
paid off your debts.

To calculate your net worth, add up your
assets—that is, what you own. For
most people, their house or car is the

What's the difference between a stockbroker and a registered investment
adviser, or RIA? The broker is a salesperson
who is legally required to sell you investments that suit your
needs. For this, he or she earns a commission every time there
is a transaction (a purchase or a sale of a stock or bond).

The standards for an RIA are considered to be higher than a
broker. RIAs are supposed to put the client's best interests first
(before their own) when they make recommendations. For this,
they will usually charge a fee that is a percent of your assets.

If you are looking for professional advice and want to only
pay for a consultation (compared to an ongoing fee for managing your money), check out the Garrett Planning Network.
It's at http://garrettplanningnetwork.com.

biggest part of their net worth. Assets include things like the equity in the home, savings accounts, certificates of deposit (CDs), investments, and retirement funds you built up, such as an IRA or 401(k). You might have a collection that is worth some money. Review your most recent account statements to be sure you're using up-to-date balances.

Then add up what you owe. Do you have a mortgage? Are you carrying high balances on your credit cards? Or do you owe someone who has lent you money? If you are serious about budgeting, it's important to get control of your debts. The first step is to recognize how much you owe and to whom.

Then subtract your debts from your assets. That gives you a net worth number that will help you make the best retirement choices.

Make an action plan

Once you've laid your personal numbers out on a few sheets of paper, you can see where you stand. Now you can start to make decisions. The critical question here is, are you living within your income? Or are you spending more than you are saving? And what can you change to bring things in balance?

Of course you can't change everything at once. But you can decide to take steps that will move you toward more savings. If your monthly spending exceeds your monthly income, start cutting costs right away. Identify "need to have" items and "want to have" items. Cut back your "wants" by some meaningful amount. Give yourself a number to work toward, say 30 percent.

Another important question is this one: Are my assets in the best place? Should I leave my cash in a bank account that

IT'S A FACT!

Bank accounts are insured up to $250,000 by the Federal Deposit Insurance Corporation (FDIC), the independent agency charged by Congress with preserving and promoting public confidence in the U.S. financial system. Credit Union accounts are insured by the government-backed National Credit Union Administration. Check out a bank or credit union's safety ratings on Bauer Financial's website, www.bauerfinancial.com. An independent company that analyzes banks and credit unions, Bauer also rates credit unions. The safest businesses get a five-star rating.

pays almost nothing in interest? Or do I have too many stocks that are high risk and could lose as much as they could gain?

The Magic Secret Rule of 4 Percent

When you're planning for retirement or need to start taking withdrawals from retirement funds for living expenses, how do you know what you can afford to take out without jeopardizing your savings and your future?

The rule of thumb is that you can take 4 percent out of your retirement savings every year *if you've invested in a diversified portfolio of stocks, bonds, and cash.* Say you have $100,000 put away for retirement. You can take an annual total of $4,000, with a small increase every year for inflation. The retirement portfolio should grow—on average—enough each year to pay taxes on the returns and cover what you withdraw. Studies have shown that a portfolio invested in this way has historically grown an average of 8 percent per year over the past 100 years.

Secrets of Saving

Some people seem to be naturally good at saving. They're the ones who skip the $2–$3 soft drink at a restaurant and stick with a free glass of water. Or perhaps they just work harder at saving than other people do. If money slips through your fingers, give these ideas a try.

Slash and stash

Slash your expenses—especially those you won't miss. If you reduce your monthly expenses by $20, you'll save $240 a year. Stash the cash and give it a chance to grow as part of your retirement fund. Here are some savvy ways to reduce monthly costs.

BUNDLE UP! AT&T and Comcast offer bundles of TV-phone-Internet or similar combos. Add up what these would cost separately, and see if you can save a few bucks by combining them with one provider and taking advantage of what they have to offer.

ELIMINATE CABLE Call the cable company and ask about reducing their charges. Find a competitor's rates to point out in your call, or ask to get the 6- or 12-month introductory rate. If that fails, watch TV shows on your computer—more and more people are doing that. Netflix and other companies offer video streaming. You can hook up your computer to a TV screen for easier viewing.

STRETCH OUT APPOINTMENTS You don't have to give up trips to the beauty salon for haircuts and manicures, but can you stretch them out a little? If you currently spend $50 at the salon every six weeks, you can save almost $100 in a year by stretching your appointments to every seven or eight weeks.

WATCH THE THERMOMETER In the winter, turn down the heat a few degrees during the day and even more while you're sleeping. Do the opposite with the AC in the summer.

BREW AT HOME If you regularly buy a cup of coffee, your cash is percolating out of your pocket. Make your coffee at home and take it with you in an insulated mug.

Use the envelope method

Dividing up money for monthly expenses by placing the cash into separate envelopes is a proven way to stick to your budget. Here's how to do it:

Make a separate envelope for each of your monthly expenses. Take out cash to cover them. Put your gas or transit money in one envelope, your grocery money in another, and your entertainment money in another. Use as many envelopes as you have expenses. Pay for those items or services out of the envelopes. You won't be able to go over budget because you will be out of cash.

It's usually easier to stick with your budget if you use cash instead of plastic. However, if you have to use a credit card, put the receipts in an envelope every month. Keep a list of what you've spent on the outside of the envelope, so you can track whether you have stayed within your budget.

Bank on it

If you're paying bank fees for a checking or savings account, that's another expense you can easily cut. Banks have traditionally offered free checking to seniors, often beginning as early as age 50 or 55. There are thousands of banks and options from which to choose. Look around—you should be able to find a bank that lets you stash your cash without paying for the privilege.

The Rule of 72

If you have been a saver, you have experienced the rewards of compound interest. Put $100 in the bank at 5 percent interest, leave it there for 10 years, and you'll have $163. The Rule of 72 will help you figure out how quickly you can double any amount of money at any percent interest. This is the equation: 72 divided by interest rate = number of years it takes to double your money. Here's an example: If you are earning 6 percent interest on your savings, divide 6 into 72, and you get 12, the number of years it will take to double your money.

To compare larger banks, use www.findabetterbank.com. Enter your zip code and answer a few questions about your banking practices and the features that are important to you. It provides a list of banks based on your input.

Be sure to ask a lot of questions before you sign up or switch banks. There may be hidden fees, so request a fee schedule that includes such items as charges for overdrafts and stop payments. Find out if there is a minimum balance requirement, too. You will also want to know all about their ATM network—how many they have, where they are located, and whether there is a charge for using it or for using an out-of-network ATM. Until you add up everything, you won't know for sure if the bank is a good deal—or the best one for you.

In addition to traditional brick-and-mortar banks (and don't forget smaller, community banks where you may receive more personal service), also consider online banks and credit unions. Online-only banks can offer some great deals

Scam Alert!

Beware an e-mail that looks like it's from the IRS and says that you're due a tax refund. It is *not* from the IRS. The phony e-mail will ask you to send your Social Security number and bank account number. Don't do it! The message is from cyber crooks who will use your personal information to remove money from your accounts or create a false identity. The use of phony e-mails to get personal info is called *phishing*.

because they don't have expensive branch offices. Of course you have no teller to visit—everything happens online.

Credit unions offer low-cost checking, savings, and loans to their members, who belong based on some common association, such as place of employment or military service. You must join the credit union; typically membership is about $15, which entitles you to vote as well as to receive dividends if the credit union earns surplus funds.

One drawback to credit unions is that they often lack an ATM network. Be sure to ask whether there is an ATM setup before signing on.

Senior Tax Relief

If you're a senior on a fixed income, paying taxes of any kind can be especially tough. Here's how to get some relief.

PROPERTY TAX If you own your own home, you pay property taxes, and the money goes to your local government. The rules vary from one city and state to another, but there is a good chance that you can qualify for a senior discount of some kind. Be sure to ask the agency that sends your tax bill.

There might be more than one opportunity to get a discount. For instance, in Cook County, Illinois, seniors can qualify for one or more of the following discounts: The "senior freeze" plan, in which the assessment does not rise as fast as it would otherwise; the Long-time Occupant Homestead Exemption for people who have lived in their homes for more than 10 years and meet certain income requirements; and the "senior citizen tax deferral," which allows lower-income seniors to put off paying property taxes until the home is sold or the owner dies (it includes a 6 percent interest charge).

If you own the home you live in, you might also be able to get a break called the homeowner's exemption. In Cook County, seniors get an additional $250 off their tax bill, over and above the usual $750 homeowner's deduction. (Landlords do not get a homeowner's exemption, except for the homes they live in themselves.)

Bottom line: It pays to call and talk with your local agency.

One way to save on taxes is to cluster tax-deductible expenses into one year so your deduction will be higher. For instance, if you spend more than a certain percentage of your income on medical costs—7.5 percent in 2011—you can deduct them on your income tax. Those expenses can include items that Medicare doesn't cover, such as dental work, eyewear, and hearing aids.

Other expenses that can be clustered include charitable giving. AARP's website even has a Charitable Giving Calculator to help you figure out your tax savings. Go to www.aarp.org and enter "Charitable Giving Calculator" in the search box.

SALES TAX Ka-ching! Every time the cash register rings, you pay a little extra to your state and local government—that is, unless you live in one of the five states with no sales tax: Oregon, Montana, New Hampshire, Delaware, and Alaska. To avoid sales tax without having to move out of state, many people make purchases over the Internet. You generally are not charged sales tax on the web unless the company has a physical entity in your state. However, states are increasingly looking at taxing Internet sales as a way to raise revenues, so this sales-tax–free shopping may disappear.

"SIN" TAXES If you smoke or drink alcohol, you are paying extra taxes for the privilege. Lawmakers love to raise revenue by increasing taxes on these items. You can look for a cheaper place to purchase smokes or alcohol, but cutting down or quitting is the only way to substantially reduce the financial burden imposed by these taxes.

INCOME TAX There are always calls for simplifying the income tax code, but every year brings more complicated rules instead. Here's how to keep your taxes down: Find free tax help at senior centers, local social service or government agencies, and even libraries. You can also check these out:

■ The IRS has a program called VITA (Volunteer Income Tax Assistance) for people who earn a max of $49,000. Call 800–906–9887 to find a location that will be in a shopping mall, library, or other accessible spot.

■ AARP offers tax assistance to seniors of low and moderate income via a program called Tax-Aide. Find information about it and other tax help at www.aarp.org.

■ Try Turbo Tax at http://turbotax.intuit.com/. It's free if your taxes are not complicated and you use the simple form.

Save Well, Sleep Well: Managing Credit and Debt

If you are one of the millions who have slipped into debt, don't give up. Seek help from a nonprofit credit counselor and get a plan in place.

Pay down credit card debt

If you are buried under a pile of bills, you can dig yourself out. What you need to do is renegotiate. Start by calling customer service for each company that is sending you bills. Tell them that you can't pay the entire bill but want to pay a certain percentage—25 percent, for example. You might need to work on this project for a few days, talking up the line of supervisors. Other folks have reached agreements with companies, and so can you.

Make a plan. Write a list of your debts, including the amount owed on each and the interest rate that you're paying for each. You will need to decide which to focus on— whether you will start paying off the biggest one first or the one with the highest rate. Experts suggest what they call the "snowball" approach: Start with the smallest debt first, paying only the minimum on the larger balances. Once you've paid off the smallest debt, you can use that payment to reduce the next smallest debt. As you go along, reducing balances and getting rid of each debt altogether, you have more cash to pay off the remaining debts. That's why it's

To check the legitimacy of a credit counselor or agency you're considering using, contact the Better Business Bureau.

called the snowball approach—your debt reduction picks up speed over time.

Reverse Mortgage: A Last Resort

A reverse mortgage, which is a loan from a bank or other financial institution, will allow you to stay in your house and have an income. The money can be paid to you in a lump sum, as a line of credit, or in regular installments. To get one, you have to be a homeowner who is at least 62 years old. The loan must be paid back when you move or sell your home, or when you die.

Reverse mortgages are legal, but proceed with caution. Critics say the fees are high, the rules are tricky, the paperwork is complicated, and coun-

IT'S A FACT!
In 2010, reverse mortgages were used by 477,567 home-owners.

selors, who are often paid a commission for every reverse mortgage they create, don't always have your best interests at heart. It's likely they won't want to disclose all aspects of the transaction, including fees and risks. As in most businesses, some lenders and representatives are "unscrupulous."

Here's what to consider:

■ As long as you keep the reverse mortgage, interest is adding up,

One of the complaints about reverse mortgages is the high fees that are charged up front. The rules have changed, though, so if you borrow less than the full amount that you're entitled to, you can save on the mortgage insurance fees.

even though you aren't making payments. What that means is the amount you owe increases over time.

■ Rates and terms will vary depending on the lender, so shop around. Likewise, get professional advice to be sure that you completely understand the terms of the deal.

■ You won't be making housing payments, but you will have to pay other home-related expenses. These include property taxes, insurance, and association fees. And you have to keep up with repairs.

Wheels of Fortune

Most people love the freedom that comes with a car, but owning a car is not cheap, and neither is buying one. Seniors have advantages when it comes to managing costs, especially when it comes to insurance.

Save on insurance

As a senior, your lifestyle and a good driving record can make a big difference to an insurance company. Here's what you have going for you:

■ If you're not driving to work, that cuts insurance prices.

■ An older car means lower insurance rates.

■ If you drive fewer miles during the year than you used to, you should get a rate reduction.

■ Good credit ratings help too.

Stretch your gas-buying dollar

The price of gas is a fact of life, but it's even harder to manage your expenses when prices go up—sometimes very fast. Besides leaving the car in the garage, what can you do to keep your costs down?

- Buy gas during the week. Try Tuesday or Wednesday. Prices go up on weekends when commuters have more time to fill the tank.

- Keep your eye on www.gasbuddy. com. It's the most well-known of the websites that track gas prices. Neighbors report prices that they've spotted, and then the prices are posted on the website. Some local radio stations provide the same service on the air.

- Don't idle. Experts say that sitting in your car with the motor running will use up gas much faster than if you turn off the engine, even if it's just for a minute or two.

- Keep up with maintenance.

Sell the car

You might not even need to own a car. If you live near public transportation or like to bike or walk, you can get a lot of errands done without driving. If you do need a car and have access to services like ZipCar and IGo that rent inexpensively by the day, you can get your hands on the wheel when you have the need.

> **SENIOR SECRET**
>
> Taking a safe driver class for seniors may reduce your car insurance rate. Many companies reward seniors with a discounted rate after they take an approved class. AARP offers online classes or at various locations. Check www.aarp.org for more information.

Protecting Your Money

Investing and using your savings wisely are the foundation of a relaxed retirement. There are lots of ways that unscrupulous folks may try to separate you from your money. Here's how to protect yourself.

Work with a professional. Everyone has a unique financial situation. An experienced advisor should be able to help clients save money and invest wisely. If you want professional help, follow these tips for finding an advisor who is right for you.

- Start by asking a lawyer or accountant if he or she can refer you to a dependable financial expert.

- Talk with friends who seem to be in good financial shape. They may be able to refer you to someone they know.

- Take a look at the advisor's title. A CFP (Chartered Financial Planner) is highly respected. CFPs take classes, have to pass a difficult test to get certified, and have promised to put their clients' best interests ahead of their own. On the other hand, some titles—"senior counselor" is one—sound good but mean nothing.

- Make an appointment for a no-fee, no-obligation meeting. Every investment professional should be willing to meet with you. Have a list of questions ready and insist on getting answers to all of them. Ask about the person's credentials and experience. Talk about how the fees work, and get the information in writing. Find out how often you will receive reports on your investments (should be every month) and how often they expect to meet with you during the year. Finally, ask for the names and phone numbers of two or three current clients. If you don't get satisfactory answers to your questions or if you feel uncomfortable at any point in the interview, cross the person off the list and move on.

- Check for known fraud. You can find out if an advisor has been in trouble in the past. For stockbrokers, go to www.finra.org, the investors section, and find BrokerCheck.® You should also check the Securities and Exchange Commission at www.sec.org. Go to the Investor Information section and from the list of links choose "Check Out Brokers & Advisors." You can look at data by the name of a firm and the individual's name.

Don't Become a Victim

There are a lot of swindlers out there who want to get their hands on your money. And they have countless ways in which to do that.

Not only that, but they are endlessly inventive. They keep dreaming up new ways to separate you from your bank account.

How do these con artists get away with it? For one thing, they prey on people who are vulnerable. Those who have lost a spouse, moved, or been downsized are especially at risk. The bad guys are very good on the phone. They talk seniors into revealing personal information—kids' names, occupation, location of bank accounts. They know how to flatter people ("Gee, you must be proud of your three grand-kids."). Soon, they are the senior's "friend," and they have set up their target to write a check for a phony purpose.

How can you spot the criminals?

- If someone you don't know asks you to write a check for any purpose, be suspicious.
- If a stranger gets in touch out of the blue—that is, he calls you, mails you, e-mails you, or knocks on your door, it should raise a red flag of doubt.

■ If you are guaranteed a return on your investment, don't sign up. Remember, there are no guarantees in life—and that is especially true for investments.

■ If you're looking into a work-at-home arrangement and you're asked to send money for a "startup kit" or "information," don't do it. Work-at-home scams are very common, especially when the economy is bad and more people are looking for jobs.

■ If someone rings your doorbell and points out that the shingles on your roof are loose, decline his help. The guy will offer to fix them now if you'll write a check for [fill in the blank] dollars. If you take him up on the offer, when he gets up on your roof, he may actually do some real damage, which he'll then charge you more to "repair."

These scams work because someone trusted the con artist. As the saying goes: If it seems too good to be true, it probably is.

Where to get help

If you believe you've been scammed, or you know someone who has, turn to these officials.

■ There is a good chance your local police department has an officer dedicated to frauds.

■ The attorney general of your state has the power to pursue scammers.

■ If mail is involved, report the scam to the U.S. Postal Inspection Service.

■ You can get general information from the Federal Trade Commission (www.ftc.gov), which is dedicated to protecting American consumers.

A Working Retirement

Many seniors do not have enough savings for retirement. Some have been unexpectedly downsized at work before they were ready to retire, and others have lost their savings to the collapse of the housing and stock markets. If you are one of those seniors, you may have decided to keep working or to find a job.

Cast a wide net

There are myriad resources to help with your job search. Make the local library your first stop, where a librarian can steer you in the right direction. Many libraries devote entire sections to employment information. They'll have books by the U.S. Department of Labor that reveal what certain jobs involve, lists of local employers in your community, and advice on résumés and interviews. Sometimes libraries will host an expert speaker or a networking group. Be sure to take advantage of all the free assistance that your library offers.

REACH OUT Get the word out that you're looking for a job. Your "inner circle" of family and friends is an easy place to start. Tell them what you're looking for, and ask if they know someone who works in a place that would be a good fit for you. Use your job search as an opportunity to have

IT'S A FACT!

If you are discouraged about finding a new job, here are two statistics in which you can take heart.

- Workers over age 55 are grabbing more new jobs than any other age group!
- The unemployment rate for workers over 55 is 3.1 percent. For all adults over age 16, unemployment is 8.8 percent.

coffee and catch up with a friend or acquaintance whom you haven't seen in a long time.

NETWORK ONLINE Social networking is a newer path to connecting with potential employers and people who can alert you to job openings. It's worth learning the ropes and using LinkedIn® and Facebook®. Combined, their networks include more than 700 million users, and they can help match job seekers with employers.

SEARCH YOUR OWN COMMUNITY Most small businesses don't have human resource departments, so it's easier to contact a decision-maker directly. Watch the local paper for start-ups or businesses that are growing, and get in touch with them.

POST YOUR RESUMÉ ON THE INTERNET There are countless job search sites on the Internet; look for those that specialize in your area of interest. Post your résumé. All the big job-search sites, such as www.monster.com, let you create a profile and publish your résumé. To get noticed on the Internet, include key words that employers want to see. Since they use technology to search through thousands of résumés, you must use terms that the search engine can identify. Take a look at key words that people with similar work backgrounds have included, and work them into your copy.

SENIOR SECRET

The trend is up. The percent of seniors who want to work in the labor force continues to increase. In 2001, about 33 percent of seniors saw themselves in the labor force. By 2011, about 40 percent of seniors said they were in the labor force. So employers are used to seeing older job applicants and workers.

2 Social Security

You worked for it, now make it work for you

When you opened your first paycheck 40 or more years ago, it probably was smaller than you expected, thanks to deductions for Social Security. You may have groused about that at the time, thinking of all you could do with the money that was being withheld. Retirement? That was too far down the road to fathom.

But now the time has come for those payroll deductions to pay off. Sounds great, right? It can be, but don't rush to sign up for Social Security benefits before you get the scoop. What you don't know can hurt you—in your pocketbook.

It's All in the Timing

You can start receiving Social Security benefits anytime between age 62 and your 70th birthday. You are the decider. The longer you wait to sign up, the larger your Social Security check will be. Benefits are the smallest at age 62 and gradually increase each month until you start taking benefits or turn 70—whichever comes first.

How much you lose if you take early retirement benefits—or gain if you wait—depends on the year you were born. The Social Security Administration (SSA) estimates that your benefit is reduced about one-half of one percent for each month you start receiving benefits before you reach full retirement age. For example, if your full retirement age is 66 but you sign up to receive benefits at 62, you will only get 75 percent of your full benefit.

At 70, you've reached the maximum amount, so there is no reason to wait any longer.

Know What Full Retirement Means

Don't get tripped up by Social Security Administration (SSA) terminology. It's important to know what full retirement means or you might accidentally take benefits before you have the need.

Here's your guide to SSA terms:

■ Early retirement: age 62, the earliest that you could qualify to take SS benefits, until your full retirement age

■ Full retirement: age 66 if you were born between 1943 and 1954. Full retirement age used to be 65, but the SSA has been gradually increasing the full retirement age starting with people born in 1938 and ending with people born in 1959. The full retirement

Once you hit age 62, you can sign up anytime. You're not limited to the three key ages of 62, 66, and 70. For example, you can sign up at age 63 and 3 months.

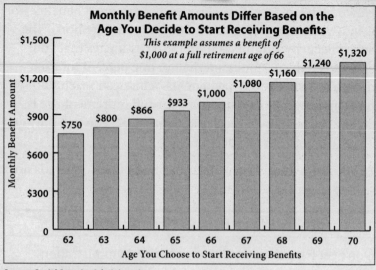

Monthly Benefit Amounts Differ Based on the Age You Decide to Start Receiving Benefits

This example assumes a benefit of $1,000 at a full retirement age of 66

Monthly Benefit Amount

Age	Amount
62	$750
63	$800
64	$866
65	$933
66	$1,000
67	$1,080
68	$1,160
69	$1,240
70	$1,320

Age You Choose to Start Receiving Benefits

Source: Social Security Administration

age for people born in 1960 or after is 67. For a chart showing full retirement age according to birth year, visit www.ssa.gov/pubs/retirechart.htm.

■ Delayed retirement: waiting beyond your full retirement age to sign up for benefits. Social Security benefits are increased by a certain percentage, depending on your date of birth, for every month that you delay taking benefits up to age 70.

Making a Wise Choice

There are some basic concepts that can help you decide when it's best for you to take Social Security benefits.

Why take early retirement?

If you can get a bigger check by waiting, then why not put off filing for your Social Security benefit? It really depends on your finances. You may not feel that you have that option. If you are no longer working, either by choice or by chance, and don't have sufficient savings or a pension, then a monthly Social Security check can help you afford necessities like rent or mortgage payments and medical care.

That's not the only reason to take Social Security early, though. Here are others:

- You are in poor health and are not sure whether you will live past your mid-70s.
- You are good at saving money and want to put your Social Security income into a conservative investment.

"Full retirement age" does not mean the age at which you get the most money. To receive the biggest possible monthly check, hold off until age 70—or as long as you can up until that age.

Why wait?

One word: Money. The most important reason to wait is that your check will increase each month and year. It may even double if you wait from age 62 to age 70.

Another word: Employment. If you are working and take Social Security before full retirement age, your benefits may be reduced, depending upon how much you earn. You're allowed to earn a certain amount of money each year before deductions are taken from your benefit. The

IT'S A FACT!

The reduction in benefits for early retirement will be even greater in the future, as the full retirement age increases.

amount changes annually, depending on the cost-of-living index. For example, if you earned more than $14,160 from your job in 2011, your Social Security benefits would be reduced by $1 for every $2 you earn over that amount.

Social Security 101

In school, you get credits for the number of classes you take. With Social Security, you get credits for each year of work that you pay into Social Security, as long as you earn the minimum amount required in that year.

To qualify, you must have 40 work credits by the time you reach the age of 62. In 2011, wage earners get one credit for every $1,120 in earnings covered by Social Security. Since 1978, workers can earn up to four work credits every year, so if you earn $4,480, you get the maximum four credits for that year.

Once you qualify with the 40 work credits (typically 10 years if you work full time year-round), the SSA will figure the size of your check. The formula used takes into account your entire work history, selecting the highest 35 years of earnings. Wages from your younger years are adjusted for inflation. If you haven't worked a total of 35 years, the years you didn't work count as zero.

Not everyone qualifies for Social Security benefits, even with 35 years or more of employment. If you

IT'S A FACT!

Before 1978, Social Security credits were earned on a quarter system. For every three months in a calendar year that you earned at least $50, you were given a quarter of coverage. Since 1978, Social Security credits are based on your annual earnings, for a maximum of four credits per year.

are or have been a teacher or other state or local government employee, you may have paid into a pension plan instead of Social Security. In that case, you will be covered by your state or local pension plan. Some people pay into both systems and so are covered by both. To explore how you fit into this equation, check with the administrator for your state. Contact info is at www.ncsssa.org/statessadminmenu.html.

Signing up for Social Security

Once you've made your decision about *when* to start Social Security, signing up is easy.

You can sign up online at www.socialsecurity.gov or in person at your local Social Security office. Or you can call Social Security at 800–772–1213. If you call, you'll have a chance to ask questions. Depending on your situation, you may be asked to provide documents, such as a birth certificate or divorce decree.

Social Security suggests that you sign up about three months before you would like to start receiving benefits.

If you and your spouse have reached your full retirement age (66 for most people), you both can claim benefits. But this isn't always the wisest approach. Depending on your situation, it may make sense just to claim benefits based on a spouse's or ex-spouse's benefit rather than your own retirement benefit. That way, you will continue to add up delayed retirement credits for your own Social Security record. Later, you can file for benefits based on your own record. Your check will be higher that way.

How to Get the Biggest Check

The size of your Social Security check will depend mostly on how much money you earned over your lifetime. If you are married, your spouse's lifetime earnings will be a factor. Here is how the amount of your benefit is figured:

MARRIED OR CIVIL UNION PARTNERS If you are married and both of you worked and are entitled to Social Security on your own, your Social Security income is based on the earnings of both. The spouse who earned the most will receive his or her full benefit. The other spouse receives benefits based on his or her earnings OR 50 percent of the benefits from the higher-earning spouse, *whichever is greater.* If one spouse has no Social Security earnings or never worked, the benefit for him or her is an additional 50 percent of the wage-earner's benefit.

DEATH If your spouse dies while you are receiving Social Security benefits, you will continue to receive a benefit. The benefit will be whatever is largest—your spouse's benefit or your own. But you won't get both.

DIVORCE If you are divorced and your ex earned more than you did, you qualify for his or her Social Security benefits if you were married for at least ten years and have not remarried—even if your ex did remarry. You must be at least 62 years old and your ex must qualify for Social Security benefits, even if he or she has not yet applied for them. (However, if he or she hasn't yet applied for them, you must be divorced for at least

IT'S A FACT!

When you receive Social Security benefits based on your former spouse's earnings, the benefits for your ex are not reduced.

two years to receive benefits.) If your former husband or wife dies, you can apply to receive the full amount that he or she was receiving, even if your former spouse has remarried.

What if you are eligible for a higher benefit based on your own earnings than you would receive based on your ex-spouse's earnings? You can't receive both, but you will get the amount that gives you the bigger check. These are the same rules that apply to someone who is still married when a spouse dies.

You can also choose to delay receiving your own benefits until you reach full retirement age and just receive your ex's. That way, your own retirement benefits will pay at a higher rate when you are ready to take them.

Eligible family members

Children under the age of 18—or up to 19 if they are full-time students—and adult children who are disabled can receive benefits in addition to a spouse.

How You Can Get More

Can you increase the size of your check once you've started taking Social Security? Yes you can!

For many people, the most direct way to increase the size of the Social Security check is just to keep working. This is especially true if you have not accumulated 35 years of employment. Even if you are earning a paycheck that's not as big as it used to be, there is a good chance you can increase the average that the SSA uses to calculate your benefits.

Here's what the Social Security administration says: "As long as you keep paying FICA and Self-Employment taxes, you can potentially keep increasing your benefit."

COST OF LIVING INCREASE Since 1975, Social Security has given COLAs—cost-of-living allowances—to help seniors keep up with rising prices. COLAs are based on the Consumer Price Index, which tracks the costs of typical items you might buy—like groceries and clothing.

There was not much overall inflation in 2009 and 2010, so there was no increase in Social Security's COLA, and seniors did not get a raise. In 2008, however, the COLA was 5.8 percent, while in 2007, seniors saw a more typical 2.3 percent increase in their Social Security checks.

Of course, if your Social Security check is increased with a COLA, you probably won't have more money in your pocket because prices for the things you buy will have gone up, too.

Keep It Safe and Convenient

Not too long ago, bad guys made it their business to know when Social Security checks were delivered. They would steal checks directly from seniors or from their mailboxes.

Today, you do not have to worry about someone walking off with your Social Security check because there are other, safer ways than the USPS to get your check—right on payment day. You can receive your money electronically in these three ways:

1. **Direct deposit to your checking account.** Sign up for direct deposit by contacting the Social Security Administration, a bank, or a credit union. You'll need to supply the routing number of your bank and your personal account number. (The routing number is the nine-digit number at the bottom-left of your check; the personal account number follows after a space.) You'll also be asked

Scam Alert!

Protect that number! Your Social Security number is like a magic key that opens many doors. No one knows this better than identity thieves or others who want to take advantage of your finances and your life. It is critical to take every possible step to keep your Social Security number private and safe.

Here are some tips :

■ Keep your card at home. Memorize the number—that's all you really need. With just a few exceptions, you do not need to show your card to anyone.

■ Watch for fraud. If your Social Security earnings record is not what you think it should be, or if you get tax forms that don't make sense, contact the SSA. Your number may have been stolen.

■ Don't give out your Social Security number just because you're asked. Find out why it is needed.

■ Shred old papers that have your SS number on them. If you don't have a shredder, cut the paper into a few pieces and toss them into the garbage at different times or places.

to specify whether your account is checking or savings. Watch your account carefully for the first month or two. It might take a while for the change to take place.

2. **Direct Express.**® You can also set up a direct deposit with a debit card called Direct Express.® Social Security will deposit your benefit check straight into the card's account, and you can use the card to pay for anything for which you would use a debit card. You can use the card at retail stores, to get cash back with purchases, or to make cash withdrawals at

banks or credit unions. You are allowed to make one ATM withdrawal a month at no charge. Most Direct Express® transactions are free, and you pay no sign-up or monthly fee. To arrange for a card and free customer service, call 888–544–6347. Free customer service is also available online at the website. Not everything is free, however. There are fees for making more than one ATM withdrawal each month, getting a paper statement mailed to you, replacing a lost card more than once each year, and some international transactions.

3. **Electronic Transfer Account (ETA)** ETAs are low-cost accounts for those who receive federal payments of any kind, including Social Security. It is a federally insured account in which you can receive electronic payments. It is specifically designed for people who don't currently have a bank account.

With an ETA, your money is available for you to use as soon as it is deposited, just as it would be if you had a bank account. And the account doesn't cost more than $3.00 a month. Creditors are not allowed to take Social Security funds out of your ETA account, so your payments cannot be garnished unless you owe child support or alimony.

ETAs are available all over the U.S., but not every bank or credit union

> IMPORTANT! Social Security is going electronic. There won't be any more paper checks after March 1, 2013. After that date, you will have to select one of the three options discussed above to have your payment deposited automatically.

Did You Know?

- 99 percent of Social Security contributions are returned in benefits, with only 1 percent going to administrative costs.

- In 2010, 54 percent of retired Americans said that Social Security is a major source of income.

- In 2011, more than 54 million Americans will receive $730 billion in Social Security benefits.

- Women make up 60 percent of Social Security beneficiaries, and they depend more heavily on Social Security than men do for income in retirement.

- Of people receiving Social Security, almost one-quarter of married couples and almost one-half of unmarried persons rely on Social Security for 90 percent or more of their income.

has an ETA. Go to www.eta-find.gov/SearchZip.cfm to find one in your area. For more information, call 888–382–3311 or call Social Security at its main number.

Decoding the Social Security Number

If you have always wondered how the Social Security number is determined, there is less to it than you think!

Every nine-digit SSN has three sets of numbers separated by dashes. The dashes make it easier to read.

The first three numbers are the only ones that have real meaning. Until 1975, the first three numbers were assigned to the state where the application came from. But even that didn't mean much, since someone could have been born in

Ohio and applied in Oregon. The numbers wouldn't indicate whether the person lived in Oregon or was just passing through.

The middle two numbers are assigned based on a rotation set up by Social Security, but they have no special meaning. The last four numbers are assigned in the order in which the application was received.

Any number beginning with 000 will NEVER be a valid SSN.

Uncle Sam Wants His Share

You may owe taxes on your benefits! Now that you've gotten yourself all set up with Social Security, be prepared to send some cash back to the U.S. government. Social Security is taxed if your income is over a certain level. Here's how it works.

- If you're single and your "combined income" is under $25,000, you don't pay any taxes. Combined income is your adjusted gross income plus any nontaxable interest income plus half your Social Security income.

- If you're married and file a joint return with a combined income of less than $34,000, you won't pay taxes.

- If your combined income is over these amounts, you will pay income tax on 50 to 85 percent of your Social Security benefit. Check with a tax advisor for your personal situation.

Supplemental Security Income

If you haven't met the requirements for Social Security, check out the Supplemental Security Income (SSI) program.

It makes payments to people with low income who are age 65 or older or are blind or have some other disability.

Start your SSI application on the Social Security website: www.socialsecurity.gov. Or call 800–772–1213 to set up an appointment at a Social Security office.

Expect to bring a lot of paperwork to your meeting! Your representative will want to see items such as your Social Security card, birth certificate, mortgage papers or lease, payroll records, bank books, and medical records.

Whether you will be approved for SSI depends on your income and your resources.

Income is money you receive, such as wages and pensions. You are allowed to have a very small amount of income from another source and still receive SSI. When deciding whether you will get SSI, Social Security allows you to keep part of the income you receive from working, and it does not count food stamps. If you are married, Social Security considers your spouse's income in making the decision.

> **IT'S A FACT!**
>
> The basic SSI amount is the same nationwide, but many states add money to the basic benefit. You can call the Social Security office to find out the amounts for your state.

The amount of income you can receive each month and still get SSI depends partly on where you live because limits vary by state.

Resources are things you own, such as real estate, bank accounts, cash, stocks, and bonds. If you are single and your resources are worth no more than $2,000, you may be able to get SSI. For couples, resources should not be greater than $3,000. Some items don't count as resources. Your home and the land it is on, your car (usually) and burial plots for you and your immediate family are not part of the $2,000/$3,000 benchmark.

Get Other Benefits Too

If you are getting SSI, you might be able to get more help from these other government sources.

■ Medicaid. You may also be able to get Medicaid to help pay for doctor and hospital bills. Your local welfare or medical assistance office can give you information about Medicaid.

■ Medicare. It's possible that your state will pay your Medicare premiums and, in some cases, other Medicare expenses such as deductibles and coinsurance.

■ Social Security. If you worked and paid into Social Security, you could also receive Social Security benefits at the same time as SSI. Retirement benefits can be paid to people age 62 or older and their families. Disability benefits go to people with disabilities and their families.

> **IT'S A FACT!**
>
> Social Security paid a monthly benefit of $1,177 to the average worker at the beginning of 2011. Because the total amount of benefits changes all the time, and so do the number of people receiving benefits, this average changes every month.

3 Get the Most from Medicare

Medicare—the federal government's health insurance program for people age 65 and older, some disabled people, and those with end-stage renal disease—is the backbone of medical coverage for older Americans. Nearly 40 million people are covered by it. Yet negotiating the Medicare maze can be complicated, frustrating, and time-consuming.

Do You Qualify?

Compared to the many decisions and choices you will need to make once you are in the Medicare program, the rules to qualify for it are pretty simple:

■ You can start Medicare when you are 65 years old.

■ You must be a U.S. citizen or a permanent legal resident.

IT'S A FACT!

Medicare is actually part of the U.S. government's Social Security Administration. When you use one or both of the programs, it seems that they are separate, and for the most part they are. But once in a while, you come across an exception, as you will see on the next page. As a general rule, you need to have worked long enough to qualify for Social Security in order to get Medicare benefits.

- You or your spouse must have worked long enough to qualify for Social Security. If your spouse is deceased or you are divorced, you still may qualify. People with Railroad Retirement Board benefits also qualify.

If you have a recognized disability, then you may be able to start Medicare early. Disabled people who have received disability benefits from Social Security for 24 months or more can start Medicare before age 65. Likewise, if you have Lou Gehrig's disease or kidney failure, or if you are receiving a disability pension from the Railroad Retirement Board, you may qualify for an early start. Check with the Medicare office to find out.

> If you don't qualify for Medicare because your work record is not long enough, you might qualify based on your spouse's or your ex's record. You also may be able to join the program by paying a higher rate.

It's Your Move

The phone is not going to ring when it's time to sign up for Medicare!

If you are already receiving Social Security benefits, Medicare will contact you a few months before you are eligible. If you are living in the United States, you will automatically be enrolled in Part A, which covers hospital stays, and Part B, which covers outpatient services. However, you can choose to reject Part B coverage.

If you have not yet started Social Security—and remember, full retirement age for Social Security is 66—you must get in touch with Medicare to get the ball rolling. *Contact Medicare three months before your 65th birthday.*

If you wait and fail to contact Medicare as suggested, your coverage can be delayed by one to three months. If you delay too long (what constitutes "too long" depends on the particular circumstances), you could also be hit with higher premiums.

To speak with a representative, call Medicare at 800–772–1213 on weekdays from 7 A.M. to 7 P.M. At other times, you will reach Medicare's automated response, and you might be able to get help that way. You can also get lots of information online at www.medicare.gov or by visiting a Social Security office to speak with an agent in person.

Once a year, Medicare will send you a book called *Medicare & You.* This is your guide to what Medicare will cover.

Medicare's 4-Letter Alphabet

Since the Prescription Drug Plan was added to the Medicare Program in 2006, there are four parts to Medicare, each with a different purpose. Not everyone uses every part. The following are Medicare's building blocks.

PART A This covers overnight stays in a hospital, as well as costs such as tests and doctors who take care of you while you are there. It can also cover a stay in a skilled nursing facility for up to 100 days if the situation meets Medicare rules. If you leave the skilled nursing facility for 60 days, the 100-day allowance can start over. Medicare does not cover long-term care in a nursing home. Part A also covers some home health care and hospice care.

PART B This is outpatient coverage for doctors and nurses, as well as a wide range of services and products such as X-rays, tests, some vaccinations, blood transfusions, and chemotherapy. It also covers durable medical equipment that helps you move around or take better care of yourself, such as canes, walkers, wheelchairs, and oxygen tanks.

PART C This is also known as the Medicare Advantage Plan, which is a private insurance coverage option. You can sign up for an Advantage plan *instead of* Medicare's hospital insurance in Part A and doctor coverage in Part B. Many Advantage plans also cover prescription drugs so you do not need a separate Part D plan. Plans may also cover some expenses for dental, vision, and hearing, as well as wellness programs. Advantage plans vary widely in cost.

What's the best way to get the max out of Medicare? With Medicare, timing is everything. If you miss an important date, you'll pay a penalty. Make sure you get all the benefits you deserve.

PART D D is for drugs, so it's easy to remember what it covers. The youngster in the Medicare alphabet, Part D was added in 2006. Part D is not required, but if you pass it up when you have the opportunity, it can be expensive to change your mind. You will pay a penalty for late enrollment. The penalty varies, but you can find a formula to estimate it, as well as other information about late enrollment, at https://questions.medicare.gov/app/answers/detail/a_id/2255/~/late-enrollment-penalty-(lep).

All the Part D prescription drug plans—and there are many!—are managed by private insurance companies. There is a wide range of costs and coverage, so you should be able to find a plan that works best for the medications you expect to need during the year. Once you've decided on a plan, you will purchase it directly from the insurance company.

If your health and prescriptions change, you can change plans once a year—or join a plan for the first time—during the open enrollment period November 15 to December 15.

Mind the Medigap

Medicare provides insurance for essential medical care that many would not be able to afford on their own. But it doesn't cover everything. There are deductibles and copays that are your responsibility. And there are some important—and expensive—services that aren't covered, including vision screening, eyeglasses, dental care, dentures, hearing aids, private-duty nursing, and long-term care. Medicare also doesn't cover you when traveling outside the United States.

If you'd like to find a way to cover the services and products that Medicare does not, consider taking out a Medigap policy (also referred to as Medicare Supplemental). Medigap is

Scam Alert!

Insurance providers may try to sell you duplicate coverage. There are laws against this, but you still should be vigilant. Check and compare your Medicare coverage with the policy that is being offered to you. If you suspect a violation, call the Inspector General of the Department of Health and Human Services on this toll-free hotline: 800–447–8477.

not part of Medicare and isn't another government program. It's health insurance sold by private insurance companies to fill the gaps in Medicare coverage.

Medicare decides what each Medigap plan offers, so they are consistent and fit with the government program. There are ten plans to choose from, each identified with a letter of the alphabet, and

> **IT'S A FACT!**
>
> There's always an exception! Three states—Massachusetts, Minnesota, and Wisconsin—have their own standardized supplemental insurance plans.

they must be identical no matter which private insurance company sells you the coverage. Plan A purchased from Metropolitan Life in Athens, Georgia, then, is identical to Plan A purchased from Farmers Insurance in Ann Arbor, Michigan. There's just one catch: Not all plans are available in every area. To find out who the Medigap providers are in your state, check the state's website.

The government does *not* determine what each plan costs, however. Different insurance companies can charge different amounts for identical plans—that's why it's so important to shop around.

Would You Like to Buy an "A"?

No matter which Medicare plans you choose, you will pay for each of them separately. Here's what each letter of the Medicare alphabet costs and covers.

PART A Hospitalization coverage. Part A is a bargain. There is no charge for Part A if you paid enough Medicare taxes while working. (If you don't qualify through the Medicare taxes you've paid, you can pay out of your own pocket to participate in Part A.) There is a deductible, though. In 2011, the deductible was $1,132. Depending on the Medicare Advantage or a Medigap plan you sign up for, the deductible may be covered.

PART B Medical Coverage. You pay a monthly premium for Part B. For most people, the cost is $96.40 or $115.40, depending upon their income. People with high incomes pay the larger amount. If you are receiving Social Security benefits, the cost for Part B is deducted from your check. If you aren't taking Social Security, Medicare will send you a bill four times a year. You also pay a deductible with Part B. In 2011 it was $162. And you are charged a copay of 20 percent of the Medicare-approved amounts for most services. If you have signed up for an Advantage Plan or Medigap, the deductible and copay may be covered or reduced by the insurance company.

PART C Advantage Plans. You will find a range of costs, as well as different rules for how you get medical services, depending on the particular type of Advantage plan you choose. Your plan may charge a monthly premium, and you may have an annual deductible as

Medicare Advantage, Medigap policies, and Part D are all private insurance plans. They are supervised by the Department of Insurance in your state. So, to start exploring which plan makes sense for you, check with your state agency. You can find contact information by starting at www.medicare.gov and clicking the Resource Locator tab.

Medicare at a Glance			
NAME	**COVERS**	**MANAGED BY**	**COST AND HOW PAID**
Part A	Hospitals	Medicare (government)	No cost to you except a deductible
Part B	Doctors	Medicare (government)	Premium paid to Medicare by checking or deducted from Social Security
Part C Advantage	A, B, and sometimes D	Private companies	Price varies; paid directly to insurance company
Part D	Prescription drugs	Private companies	Price varies depending on deductible and copay; paid directly to insurance company
Medigap or Supplemental	Deductibles and copays	Private companies	Price varies depending on deductible and copay; paid directly to insurance company

well as other deductibles. You will likely have a copay of some amount, depending on what the insurance company will cover. You will pay the insurance company directly.

PART D Prescription Drug Plan. Like Advantage Plans and Medigap, you will buy your Prescription Drug Plan from a private insurance company. There are many choices! Costs can range from about $35 to over $100 a month, depending on your deductible. (Medicare and each state can provide information to help you compare plans.)

There are actually four levels or phases to Part D every year, which vary according to the total cost of your prescriptions.

1. Annual deductible. You pay an out-of-pocket deductible up to a maximum amount ($310 in 2011). However, there is a good chance you will find a Part D plan that does not charge a deductible or one that charges less than the max.

2. Initial coverage period. You pay the copay, and the insurance company pays the rest until you reach a maximum amount for the year ($2,840 in 2011). The copay amount varies according to the plan you chose.

3. The "doughnut hole." Also called the coverage gap or the second deductible, this is a period of time during which your insurance company does not pay for or subsidize your prescription drug costs. You enter the doughnut hole when you and your insurance company have paid the maximum amount of the initial coverage period, and you stay there until you have spent a maximum amount ($4,550 in 2011), which is when you meet the catastrophic coverage requirement. Because there were so many complaints about the coverage gap, the 2010 Health Care Act provided that you get discounts on brand-name and generic drugs. Discounts increase each year, and the doughnut hole will gradually close by 2020 as the government picks up more of the tab.

4. Catastrophic coverage: If your drugs cost more than the coverage gap ($4,550 in 2011), you will pay no more than 5 percent of the cost of any prescription drug or $2.50 for covered generic drugs until the end of the year.

The next year, you start from scratch, going through each of the four phases in order.

Checking It Out

One of the great things about Medicare is that it tells you clearly what it covers and what it does not cover. There are no pre-approvals, and you can't be excluded for pre-existing conditions.

There are a number of ways to find out if Medicare will cover a particular health issue. Try these:

■ Go online to www.medicare.gov and use the search box to find the answer to your question.

■ Check the book *Medicare & You* that you receive in the mail every year.

■ Call 800–772–1213 Monday–Friday or visit a Social Security office.

Finding a doctor

Medicare sets prices that it will pay for doctor visits and medical treatments. Not every doctor wants to accept these set fees, so you will want to make sure you are working with one who has signed on with Medicare. To find a Medicare doctor, check at Medicare's website or call.

Part D, Medigap, and Advantage Plans

If you have questions regarding coverage with the plans that are managed by private insurance companies, you should contact them directly.

■ Most Medigap policies have a maximum amount of benefits they will pay within a set amount of time.

■ Some Medigap policies may not cover certain health conditions for the first six months. However, Federal law mandates that Medigap insurers cover pre-existing conditions after the six months.

What the Health Care Reform Act of 2010 Means for People with Medicare

Before the Health Care Reform Act, Medicare did not pay for preventive health care. The Reform Act shifted the emphasis to staying well, and beginning in 2011, no copay or deductible is charged for preventive services that are rated A or B by the U.S. Preventive Services Task Force. You can now get a free annual physical with a doctor who accepts Medicare reimbursement in full. Colorectal cancer screening and mammograms are free. There are also more lab tests on the list that you won't have to pay for.

In addition, the new law does the following:

- For Advantage plans, it ensures that insurance companies spend at least 85 percent of the premiums they receive on healthcare (not administrative costs).
- Increases support for community health centers.
- Helps patients return home from the hospital by connecting them with community services.
- Includes tools that protect seniors from scammers.
- Gives Medicare new tools to cut back on waste and fraud. This saves Medicare money—about $500 billion over 10 years—and those savings go into the Medicare Trust Fund.

Is Medicare on Life Support?

Estimates for Medicare's financial health change frequently. Analysts now say the Health Care Act of 2010 takes steps that will keep Medicare solvent until 2029. On the other hand, medical costs continue to rise faster than inflation.

That and other pressures mean that there will be an ongoing debate about how to strengthen Medicare's financial condition.

Medicare is the third largest government expense, after Social Security and defense. Its funds come from payroll taxes, other taxes, and premiums paid by Medicare recipients.

Medicaid: A Joint State and Federal Program

Medicaid is a program that helps low-income citizens with health care and nursing home care. The U.S. government determines the general rules and pays for a large part of the program. Each state pays up to half the remaining cost of Medicaid and manages the program in that state.

Not everyone who is poor is eligible for Medicaid. The rules can be different from state to state. Besides being below certain income and asset levels, states will look at age, disability, and pregnancy. If you are applying for Medicaid, you must prove that you are a U.S. citizen or a resident alien.

The sickest and the poorest Medicare beneficiaries are eligible for both Medicaid and Medicare. They are called dual eligibles.

If you want to find out more from your state's Medicaid program, use the Internet to search for the state name and Medicaid, such as "Ohio Medicaid." Or look in a directory for your state agency that handles health and family matters.

4 Smart Ways to Manage Medical Issues

As you may have already discovered, being a senior can mean spending more time with health care professionals. Medical problems crop up, and preventive measures are more important than ever. You'll be better able to navigate the health care system and access the best care for the least cost if you are an informed and proactive health care consumer.

Need a New Doc?

Once you're on Medicare, you will have new factors to consider when it comes to seeing a doctor. The primary care doctors or specialists that you've been using may not take Medicare. Don't wait until you have an urgent concern; find out in advance.

IT'S A FACT!

To find a doctor who accepts assignment from Medicare, go to www.medicare.gov. Click the "Resource Locator" tab at the top of the page, and then select "Doctors" from the drop-down menu. Search criteria include the doctor's specialty, zip code, and gender. You'll get a list of doctors based on your responses.

Don't hesitate to check on the doctor's reputation. One place to check credentials—licenses and education—is hosted medical boards of the 50 states. Find your state board at www.docboard.org/docfinder.html.

If any of your doctors have opted out, these are your choices:

- Look for a new doctor who always accepts Medicare assignment.

- Ask your doctor(s) about working out an affordable fee schedule privately so that you can stay in the practice. (Some doctors may be willing to negotiate; you won't know unless you ask.)

- Purchase a Medigap or Advantage plan that covers the doctor(s) you want to see (you'll need to check each name).

- Stick with your doctor and pay out of pocket for any bills the doctor sends you.

Make the Most of Your Doctor Visit

If it seems like the doctor has even less time for you than before, you're probably right. Doctors are under a lot of pressure from insurance companies and

SENIOR SECRET

You don't have to go to the doctor's office every time you need to check your blood pressure. You can do it for free at many more convenient locations. Your local hospital, drugstore, and retail chain store (such as Target) often offer free blood pressure screenings with a nurse or other health practitioner on particular days of the week or month. So do local health departments (county, townships, villages) and community colleges. Call to find out what the schedule is so you don't miss out.

Don't rely solely on free blood pressure machines that many stores provide. They are not accurate enough to make health decisions about your blood pressure.

malpractice insurers to keep costs down, and their overhead keeps going up. To handle the demands, many are trying to squeeze more patients into a day. You'll get more out of the limited time for your visit by being on time and prepared for your appointment.

PLAN AHEAD Keep a notebook of health-related information so all the information you might need is at your fingertips. Here's what your notebook should include:

- A list of medications, including when you started taking them, dosage, and frequency. Include both prescription and nonprescription medications.
- A list of tests you've had and their results
- A list of past and upcoming medical appointments
- A dated list of symptoms that you are concerned about

BEFORE YOUR APPOINTMENT Write down all the questions that you want to ask, and don't be embarrassed about referring to it.

AT YOUR APPOINTMENT Make sure the doctor knows that you have questions. Take out your list and notebook so it is visible. When it is your turn to talk, start with the most important questions. Ask the doctor to spell any unfamiliar terms or medications and to explain them. Take notes. Stay on the subject!

BRING SUPPORT If possible, take someone with you, especially if you are dealing with a life-threatening condition and all the strong emotions that go with it. A support person can take notes and think of questions that escape you—and will listen with a more objective ear. Later, you can talk about what the doctor said and what it means.

IT'S A FACT!

The value of bringing support to the doctor's office is now being recognized with a growing trend to hire a "patient advocate." In addition to providing support, an advocate might manage paperwork, arrange transportation, and do more research for you. To find a professional advocate, go to the website of the National Association of Healthcare Advocacy Consultants, www.nahac.memberlodge.com. You can search by service area to find an advocate near you.

Whom Can You Trust?

It's easy to find medical information on the Internet, but can you believe everything you read? Here are three reputable sites:

- WebMD: www.webmd.com. Besides basic information, this website also offers quizzes, calculators, guides, and self-assessments.

- Mayo Clinic: www.mayoclinic.com/health-information. The world-famous Mayo Clinic has online guides to medical conditions, each of which includes a section called "preparing for your appointment" that lists questions to ask your doctor about that particular condition. The website also has a wealth of other information.

- U.S. Government: www.health.nih.gov. You'll find just about any health issue listed here. The government sponsors scientific research and shares results with you.

Shedding Light on Providers

When it comes to general medical professionals, most people think of an internist, a family practitioner, and a nurse.

But there are many more types of health care providers you are likely to encounter during regular office visits at your general practitioner, during a hospital stay, or at an urgent care or walk-in clinic.

Don't feel gypped if you are treated by one of the following. You're likely to get more personal care from them:

DOCTOR OF OSTEOPATHY (OD) Osteopaths are medical doctors who take a holistic approach to treating their patients. Their education and training is similar to that of MDs—4 years of medical school followed by specialty training. Osteopathic doctors then receive an additional 300 to 500 hours of training in the musculoskeletal system. Many ODs use manual therapies, such as spinal manipulation and massage therapy, in their treatment. About 7 percent of physicians in the United States are osteopaths. For more information, visit the American Osteopathic Association at www.osteopathic.org.

PHYSICIAN ASSISTANT (PA) Physician assistants are trained and licensed health care professionals who practice medicine under a doctor's supervision. They give physical exams, diagnose and treat illnesses, order and interpret medical tests, advise patients on preventive care, assist in surgery, and

Scam Alert!

Beware offers of free medical products! According to the FBI, senior citizens are often the targets of Medicare fraud schemes from equipment manufacturers. These companies will offer a free medical product in exchange for a Medicare number. The scammer will fake a doctor's signature or get a corrupt doctor to sign the form and use it to bill Medicare for merchandise that was not needed or ordered.

prescribe medication. Studies show that PAs can handle about 80 percent of the conditions that are usually seen in a primary care setting. For more info, check the American Association of Physician Assistants at www.aapa.org.

NURSE PRACTITIONER (NP) Nurse practitioners are registered nurses who have completed significant advanced education and training. They must hold both a national board certification in a specialty area and state licensing through their state's nursing board. Like physician assistants, nurse practitioners can provide many of the services that doctors usually offer. They can take a patient history and perform physical exams, and they can diagnose and treat diseases. In many cases, they can prescribe medications (it depends on the state's regulations). Unlike the doctor, they can take the time to work with a patient on prevention and education with the goal of promoting a healthy lifestyle. In some states, NPs can practice independently, while in others they must work with a physician. Care provided by an NP is covered by Medicare if it is in a doctor's office, a clinic, or a hospital setting.

Walk-in and Urgent Care Clinics

These alternatives to the traditional doctor's office are cropping up all over the place. They're convenient, they're nearby, and you don't need an appointment.

They're also less expensive—and that's why their numbers are growing rapidly. It's cheaper to set a broken arm in an urgent care clinic than in a hospital emergency room. It's also cheaper for a nurse practitioner to check on a bladder infection or provide a flu vaccination than it would be for the same treatment at the doctor's office.

Walk-in clinics, also called convenient care or retail clinics, can be found in drugstores and big-box stores like Target and Walmart. They're almost always staffed by nurse practitioners and physician assistants. In some cases, doctors are also available.

Convenient care clinics treat common illnesses such as colds and flu, allergies, minor injuries, headaches, sprains and strains, bronchitis, urinary tract infections, and intestinal infections. You can also get preventive care—health screenings and vaccinations, for example—at a retail clinic.

SENIOR SECRET

If you're looking for a doctor who takes Medicare and you like a particular doctor at a walk-in clinic, you may be able to continue to see him or her. Most clinics take Medicare, but as always, it's a good idea to check with the clinic beforehand.

To locate a walk-in clinic near you, go to Convenient Care Clinics at www.ccaclinics.org.

Urgent care clinics will take care of illness and injuries that are not quite serious enough to warrant a trip to the emergency room. This helps reduce the number of patients in the emergency room, allowing nurses and doctors to focus on those with critical issues. Typically, health professionals at an urgent care clinic can take X-rays, set a simple fracture, perform minor surgery, and prescribe medication.

How do you decide where to go? "Life threatening" are the operative words here. If a health issue appears to be life threatening, call 911 and get to the emergency room. Otherwise, if you need medical help quickly, head for an urgent care clinic.

To find an urgent care clinic, check out The American Academy of Urgent Care Medicine at http://aaucm.org.

Hear, See, and Speak No Coverage

As you grow older, so do your eyes, your ears, and your teeth. They need more care, but for the most part, Medicare does not cover them. You're on your own for routine preventive care such as hearing and vision tests, and for hearing and visual aids such as hearing aids and eyeglasses. You're on your own, too, when it comes to dental care.

What Did You Say?

Many people begin to lose hearing capacity as they age. The most common type of hearing loss is called presbycusis, which is the term for age-related, or sensorineural, hearing loss. There are many causes.

Symptoms include:

■ trouble hearing higher pitches (like a 3-year-old granddaughter!), and better understanding of lower pitches (men's voices)

- difficulty in noisy places, such as restaurants
- difficulty discerning words in conversation—it sounds like people are mumbling all the time

> **IT'S A FACT!**
>
> The prefix "presby," as in presbyopia, means aging, which is why you are encountering it more frequently in diagnoses these days.

Your road to better hearing will probably start with a visit to an ear doctor—an otolaryngologist—who can tell you what type of hearing loss you have. If hearing aids will help, the doctor will refer you to a clinic and an audiologist, who is university-trained to help you manage your hearing loss and select the best hearing aid for you. The hearing aid should come with a trial period of 60 days or longer, so you can make sure that it will be helpful in most situations. Hearing aids do not work as well as a good pair of ears, but they can help you lead an active social life.

Hearing aid assistance

Cost can be a huge barrier to getting hearing aids. These are good resources:

- The Hearing Loss Association of America (HLAA) speaks up on hearing-loss issues in Washington, D.C., and provides information for people who need it. HLAA has local chapters around the country where you can meet others who share your concerns. Go to www.hearingloss.org or call 301–657–2248.

- AUDIENT is a network of top-name hearing aid providers that help low-income people get access to hearing aids and care. More than 1,000 hearing aid providers have agreed to take participants who have been qualified by AUDIENT. You can find more information and an application form at www.audientalliance.org, or call 866–956–5400 (ask for AUDIENT).

■ The Foundation for Sight & Sound helps people with limited income get access to hearing aids through its Help America Hear Program. For information and an application, go to www.foundationforsightandsound.org/help_america_hear_program.html.

■ Starkey, which manufactures hearing aids, has the Hear Now Program to assist people who are deaf or hard of hearing and have no other resources to acquire hearing aids. The company also has a hearing aid recycling program. It takes donations of hearing aids of any age, make, or model. The donations are tax deductible. You can go to www.starkeyhearingfoundation.org/hear-now.php or call either 866–354–3254 (Midwest) or 310–691–1411 (West Coast).

Oh Say, Can You See?

You've no doubt already discovered that your eyes change as the birthdays roll around. Some changes are merely inconvenient while others require surgical intervention. These are the most common eye issues:

■ Presbyopia: Difficulty focusing on objects that are close. The first sign of this may be trouble reading a menu or ingredients listed on food products. At first, drugstore magnifiers or reading glasses may suffice, but as the condition worsens, you'll likely need prescription lenses.

■ Cataracts: Cloudiness in the eye's lens. Symptoms can include blurry or fuzzy vision, increased glare from lights (particularly from oncoming headlights at night), and poor central vision. More than 22 percent of Americans have cataracts. Surgery is recommended when cataracts affect daily quality of life.

■ Night and low-light vision: It's not your imagination! People in their 60s need about three times as much light to read easily as do 20-year-olds.

Regular eye checkups are crucial for detecting and treating more serious age-related conditions. Glaucoma, macular degeneration, and diabetic eye disease can all cause blindness but don't necessarily have warning signs or symptoms.

Eyewear on a budget

Medicare covers cataract surgery and eyeglasses postsurgery, but in most other cases, you're on your own when it comes to getting eyeglasses. Here are options for those on a budget:

■ New Eyes for the Needy works with opticians around the United States who donate their services and eyeglasses to people who need them. You can apply online at www. neweyesfortheneedy.org.

IT'S A FACT!

Keep these pointers in mind when you're choosing eyeglasses.

■ If you have the whiter/lighter hair and paler skin that comes with the senior years, pick frames in pale colors that don't overwhelm your face.

■ If you have a strong prescription that calls for thicker lenses, try the new high-tech materials. They are lighter weight and thinner.

■ Get UV coating. Ultraviolet coating can help prevent sun exposure, which has been linked to the development of cataracts and other eye diseases.

■ EyeCare America is a foundation run by the American Academy of Ophthalmology. More than 7,500 eye doctors volunteer their services for people age 65 and over who are in need. You can apply online at www.eyecareamerica.org or call 800–222–3937.

> **IT'S A FACT!**
>
> If you are a veteran, the VA offers services to vets with eye diseases and injuries. Go to www.veteranseyecare.com to find out more. There's an eye-care facility locator on the site to help you find a nearby veterans' eye facility.

■ Lions Club International: This service organization is dedicated to preventing blindness and providing eye care. Check with your local Lions Club to find out what services they provide.

■ Onesight.org partners with local charitable organizations and eyeware companies to offer free vision care and new eyewear. Find out more at www.onesight.org.

Healthy Teeth on a Budget

Your mouth is the gateway to your body, so keeping your teeth in good condition helps to prevent harmful bacteria from getting into your bloodstream.

Even if you faithfully brush your teeth and floss, good dental care can make a big difference in your health. If you have dental insurance from your employer, you're one of the lucky ones. It is expensive to get dental insurance if you are not employed at a company where it is offered.

Dental care on a budget

Here are some ways to take care of your teeth without breaking the bank:

GO TO SCHOOL You'll get excellent care at a reduced price—about one-third to one-half the cost at a regular dental practice—by getting treated by dental students at a dental school. Students are closely supervised by faculty, and sometimes the professor will even do the work. Another plus: They'll definitely be up to date on all the latest techniques.

The catch? You pay with your time. You may have more and longer appointments because students take longer to do their work and their supervisors will inspect it.

> **SENIOR SECRET**
>
> For regular teeth cleanings on a budget, check at the American Dental Hygiene Association www.adha.org for programs similar to those of dental schools.

If this sounds like a good deal to you, start by searching for a dental school near you. You'll find a list of more than 50 schools at the American Dental Association website, www.ada.org.

INSURANCE VS. DENTAL DISCOUNT You can buy your own dental insurance. A Delta Dental policy through AARP offers two types. Monthly premiums are $43 or $60 a month, depending on the policy, with a maximum benefit per year of $1,000 or $1,500. With root canals, implants, and bridges going for much more than the Delta Dental policy, make sure you do the math to see if this insurance will work for you.

Dental discount plans have popped up in recent years. They work differently than insurance. For starters, the monthly fee is lower—about $10–$12—and you can get connected to dentists in your area who will do your work for a discount. You agree to get the work done and pay the dentist directly—there's no middleman or insurance reimbursements.

MEDICARE AND MEDICAID By law, Medicare does not pay for what the average person would consider to be normal dental care, such as fillings and removal or replacement of teeth. In some states, Medicaid covers emergency dental care.

Uncle Sam *might* help. There is an outside chance you could obtain low-cost or free dental care as part of a clinical trial funded by the U.S. government. Clinical trials for studies of all kinds of conditions—not just dental—can be found at www.clinicaltrials.gov or call 800–411–1222. Another possibility is community health centers that provide free or reduced-cost health care, including dental. To check on this, call 888-ASK-HRSA.

Surviving a Stroke

Every 40 seconds, someone in the United States has a stroke, and the vast majority of those are first attacks. Strokes account for about 1 in every 18 deaths and are the leading cause of serious, long-term disability. Your risk of having a stroke increases with age.

If you suspect a stroke—for yourself or someone nearby—don't wait! Every second counts. Call 911, even if it seems the symptoms have passed. If you can get to the emergency room within 60 minutes of the first symptoms, you have the best chance of getting effective treatment.

Scam Alert!

The U.S. Food and Drug Administration has a list of cancer scams to avoid. Look under www.fda.gov/drugs. Then put "fake cancer cures" in the search box.

TEST FOR A STROKE A doctor came up with a simple, three-part test to help you detect whether someone is having a stroke.

1. Tell the person to smile or show their teeth. A lopsided smile or mouth indicates one-sided facial weakness—a sign of a stroke.

2. Ask the person to close their eyes and raise their arms. If both arms are not about even, it shows arm weakness—a sign of a stroke.

3. State a short sentence, and ask the person to repeat it. If they slur their words, it's a sign of a stroke.

Other stroke symptoms include trouble walking, dizziness or loss of balance, trouble speaking, confusion, numbness or paralysis on one side, and headache.

Alternative Options

Looking for alternatives to conventional medicine for solving some of your nagging health issues—or to improve your health and well-being?

You're not alone. A 2007 National Health Interview Survey of Americans found that 38 percent of adults use complementary and alternative medicine (CAM), and that number has likely grown since then.

Despite the trend, Medicare and Medicaid often don't pay for CAM treatment. What's a senior to do?

Read "Paying for CAM Treatment" on the website of The National Center for Complementary and Alternative Medicine (NCCAM). Find the arti-

IT'S A FACT!

More than 37 percent of hospitals offer one or more alternative medicine therapies.

cle at www.nccam.nih.gov/health/financial. It discusses your options, including what benefits you can receive from Medicare and Medicaid. The NCCAM, a division of the National Institutes of Health, is charged with studying the efficacy of complementary and alternative medicine. Its website offers a wealth of information. You'll find explanations of various therapies and whether they have been proven effective, information on various diseases and conditions, and the latest research and clinical trials.

5 Secrets of Healthy Aging

Diet and exercise are the best weapons against many age-related complaints and conditions. With the right kind of food and a sufficient amount of physical activity, you can stave off chronic health problems—and feel good inside and out. You'll not only live longer, you'll enjoy those years even more.

Unload the Spare

Since you turned 50, did you grow an extra layer around the middle without eating more than usual? If you are sporting a spare, you're not alone. There's a simple but not widely known reason for an increase in girth at middle age: You don't need as many calories!

During times of major growth, such as infancy and adolescence, you require more calories to support cell growth and make muscles, among other things. In fact, the calorie needs of a baby are four times the calories per pound required by someone who is 51!

IT'S A FACT!

If you eat just 100 calories more a day than you need to maintain your weight—say, the amount in two ounces of chicken or a tablespoon of peanut butter—you will pack on 10 pounds more per year unless you increase your physical activity.

Your organ systems continue to grow and develop until age 30, but then they decline by about 1 percent every year. After age 50, your body composition starts to change, and your muscle mass decreases. If you eat the same number of calories, they will settle in as fat. And if you are less physically active than before, you will burn fewer calories and pack on more pounds.

The Secret to Living Longer?

For 70 years, scientists have known that calorie restriction of 30 to 40 percent slows the aging process in laboratory animals. This restricted-calorie diet made them resistant to many age-related diseases, including cancer, heart disease, diabetes, and Alzheimer's disease—and they lived 30 to 50 percent longer.

More recently, research is showing that calorie restriction has a similar positive impact on people. So far, studies have shown that for people of normal weight, calorie restriction of about 25 percent substantially decreases the risk of "secondary aging"—diseases that accompany the aging process, such as heart disease and cancer. Whether calorie restriction in humans will also impact "primary aging," the natural accumulation of damage to cells over the years, still remains to be seen. Research continues to find out exactly what causes the increase in longevity and disease resistance, both in animals and in humans.

The average lightly or moderately active middle-aged man or woman needs about 400 fewer calories every day than when they were younger.

This much is known, though: Being overweight is detrimental to your health and your well-being. What's unknown is how much you'll enjoy the extra years you get on a calorie-restricted diet if you have to give up your favorite foods.

Eat It AND Enjoy It

Most people don't realize it, but the senses of smell and taste gradually diminish with age. So if food that you used to enjoy now seems less tasty or even bland, it's not your imagination.

Everyone knows that smell and taste are inextricably intertwined. But did you realize that the sense of smell is responsible for about 80 percent of what you taste? Unfortunately, the sense of smell begins to diminish after age 60.

IT'S A FACT!

A zinc deficiency can cause a decreased sense of taste. Ask your doctor about taking zinc supplements if a deficiency is interfering with your ability to taste food.

In fact, about half of adults over the age of 65 suffer from a diminished sense of smell. As smell goes, so goes taste.

Try these secrets to get the most pleasure from your food:

- Ask the pharmacist whether medications you are taking can interfere with your senses of taste and smell. This is a common problem and may be resolved by switching to a different drug.

- Avoid very hot foods and fluids. Heat can damage your taste buds.

- Switch often from one food to another while you're eating. Successive bites of the same food decrease your perception of its flavor.

- Don't combine foods in your mouth. That makes it more difficult to discern individual flavors and aromas.
- Vary the temperature, texture, and colors of food to enhance your enjoyment.

Don't Let Thirst Be Your Guide

Water is a vital nutrient at every age, and maintaining the proper fluid balance is critical to your health. Dehydration can wreak havoc with your body's systems, and even a small reduction in fluid intake can cause high blood pressure, circulatory disorders, kidney stones, arthritis, indigestion, and constipation.

As you get older, however, you can't rely on thirst to tell you when you need to drink more fluids. The sense of thirst, like other senses, diminishes with age. By the time you're thirsty, your body may have already lost up to 2 percent of its water weight, making you dehydrated. Dehydration can impair your ability to reason, and when the weather is warm and humid, it can cause heatstroke. Signs of heatstroke include headache, nausea, and fatigue. If you become dizzy as a result of dehydration, you increase the chance of falling and breaking a bone.

IT'S A FACT!

No matter how old you are, your body is mostly water. However, the percentage decreases with age. Babies are about 78 percent water, while senior women are about 55 percent water and senior men are about 60 percent water.

How much water you need every day depends on your environment, your level of activity, the foods you eat (some are mostly water), and even your gender. But a rule of thumb is to drink about 1.5 quarts a day. And check the color of your urine. If it is pale yellow, you are hydrated; if it's dark, then you need to drink more water.

Dementia or a Deficiency?

Your body runs on less fuel than it did before, so you need to give it premium grade for it to run optimally. The need for some nutrients increases with age, which makes a nutrient-rich diet more important than ever.

Nutrient deficiencies contribute to many age-related conditions and illnesses—and can even mimic some. Often these deficiencies go undetected and their symptoms are attributed to something else. Even a minor vitamin B_{12} deficiency, for instance, can cause memory loss and other symptoms that can be mistakenly diagnosed as dementia.

These are some of the most important nutrients that you need more of as you age:

B vitamins

The B vitamins all work together. But folate, B_6, and B_{12} in particular are crucial to support your immune system and to fight diseases and conditions to which seniors are prone, such as heart disease, stroke, dementia, and circulatory problems.

FOLATE This is the naturally occurring variety of the B vitamin found in foods such as legumes, spinach, and orange juice. Folic acid is its synthetic form, which is used to enrich food and is added to vitamin supplements. The vast majority of older adults do not get the minimum requirement of

Scam Alert!

Supplements can include ingredients that are bad for you. *Consumer Reports* found a "dirty dozen" that could actually harm seniors. Among those you should avoid: aconite, bitter orange, coltsfoot, comfrey, kava, and lobelia.

400 micrograms, putting them at risk for heart disease, megaloblastic anemia, cancer, and depression. Folate also helps preserve mental function, including the ability to make good judgments. Without adequate folate, protein production falters, affecting the growth and repair of tissues.

VITAMIN B6 Also called pyridoxine, vitamin B_6 is essential to new cell growth. It boosts the immune system, keeps blood glucose levels in check, and plays an important role in both red blood cell metabolism and protein metabolism. The best way to get sufficient vitamin B_6 is via a healthful, well-rounded diet. However, many older adults have low blood levels of B_6 because of a poor quality diet that is deficient in protein. Over time, a deficiency in vitamin B_6 can cause dermatitis, glossitis (a sore tongue), depression, confusion, and convulsions, as well as anemia.

Current Recommended Dietary Allowances (RDAs) for vitamin B_6 are 1.5 mg for women age 50 and older and 1.7 for men age 50 and older.

VITAMIN B12 Also called cobalamin, Vitamin B_{12} is essential for neurologic function and red blood cell formation, as well as for fat metabolism. It boosts energy, helps promote weight loss, and supports emotional and neurological health. It is found in many kinds of nuts, fish, dairy products, eggs, beef, pork, and organ meats such as beef liver, as well as enriched products.

Although most people get enough B_{12} from their diet, many older adults have difficulty absorbing the vitamin. As many as 30 percent of people age 50 and older—and 40 percent of those age 80 and older—have a condition called atrophic gastritis in which the body does not produce enough stomach acid to absorb the vitamin. Since so many people also take acid-reducing medications, the number of people who are deficient in vitamin B_{12} is likely higher.

Synthetic vitamin B_{12} does not require stomach acid to absorb it, so taking B_{12} supplements and eating fortified foods, such as breakfast cereal, will ensure that you get sufficient amounts of the vitamin.

A vitamin B_{12} deficiency can also be caused by a lack of intrinsic factor, a substance made in the stomach, which can cause pernicious anemia. If you have pernicious anemia, you will need vitamin B_{12} injections so that it bypasses the stomach.

Shopping for dietary supplements? Look for the USP Verified Mark. Products that carry it have been tested for quality, purity, and potency of ingredients by the U. S. Pharmacoepeia, a nonprofit voluntary standards-setting program. Visit its website: www.uspverified.org.

Most people don't realize they have a vitamin B_{12} deficiency unless they are tested for it. A deficiency can cause a range of problems, including confusion, memory loss, depression and mood swings, loss of balance, and numbness or tingling in the hands and feet, as well as fatigue, diarrhea, weight loss, and sores in the mouth.

CALCIUM AND VITAMIN D Your need for calcium increases with age—women need 200 milligrams more per day (1,200 mg total) after age 51, and men need to increase from 1,000 mg to 1,200 milligrams after age 70. However, the majority of adults do not get enough of it in their diet. Calcium is essential to keep bones and teeth strong and to prevent osteoporosis, but it also plays many other significant roles: It helps maintain healthy nerves, blood vessels, and muscles, and it is necessary for blood to clot.

Calcium does not do its job alone, however. Your body needs sufficient amounts of vitamin D—600 international units up to age 70 and 800 IU after 70—in order to absorb calcium. Recent research is finding that many adults don't have sufficient amounts of vitamin D in the bloodstream either. Your skin converts sunlight into vitamin D, but it is not as efficient at that process as you get older. Because of the long winters, people who live in the northern United States are more likely to have a vitamin D deficiency than those who live in the sunbelt. Deficiencies may also be the result of the increased use of sunscreen. Although it helps to prevent skin cancer, sunblock also prevents the skin from absorbing vitamin D.

The best source of calcium and vitamin D together is fortified, ideally fat-free or low-fat, milk. Other dairy products are also good sources of calcium but not of vitamin D. It's hard to get sufficient vitamin D in the diet if you don't drink fortified milk. Vitamin D is often added to other foods such as yogurt and breakfast cereals. It is found naturally in fatty fish and egg yolks.

If you don't get enough calcium and vitamin D in your diet, be sure to take supplements. Calcium supplements are best absorbed in doses of 500 mg or less several times throughout the day. The Institute of Medicine recommends no more than 4,000 IU of vitamin D per day, but doctors sometimes prescribe higher doses for people who have a vitamin D deficiency. Be sure to check with your doctor to find out what amount of calcium and vitamin D supplementation is right for you.

Feed Your Muscles

You've been feeding your bones calcium and vitamin D, but did you know you need to feed your muscles too? What muscles want is protein, and many older adults just aren't taking in enough to prevent a loss of muscle mass. Between 16 and 27 percent of older adults are eating less than the USDA's recommended daily allowance (RDA) of protein.

Muscles support those bones that you're so concerned about. Without muscular strength, your mobility becomes impaired. A 2007 study of 10 young and 10 elderly volunteers found that there was no difference in their ability to turn protein-rich food into muscle.

So make sure that you take in at least the RDA of protein to preserve your muscle. And exercise to strengthen the muscles that you build.

Real Folks Have the Answer

If the needle on your scale seems stuck at the same old number no matter how much you deprive yourself, you can use some weight-loss inspiration. No one knows better what works and what doesn't than people who have gone through the diet struggle themselves. Check out The National Weight Loss Registry at www.nwcr.ws. It is tracking the dieting habits of more than 5,000 people who have lost at least 30 pounds and kept it off for at least a year. Researchers want to find out what helped them lose the weight and what is helping them keep those pounds from glomming back on.

> **IT'S A FACT!**
>
> About 75 percent of American men and 68 percent of women age 60 and older are overweight or obese, according to the Centers for Disease Control and Preventions' National Health and Nutrition Examination Survey (NHANES) 2003–2006 data.

This is some of what they've discovered:

- 78 percent eat breakfast every day.
- 75 percent weigh themselves at least once a week.
- 62 percent watch less than 10 hours of TV per week.
- 90 percent exercise, on average, about 1 hour per day.

The Secret to Staying Young

You may be happy to do nothing for a while after you retire. But don't just sit there—move! Being inactive is the fastest route to aging—ungracefully. You are what you eat, for sure, but you also are what you do (or don't do).

Research continues to pile up confirming the connection between regular physical activity and good health and longevity. You probably know that exercise is good for you. But did you know it's the best way to keep your body and your mind young and supple?

You may not know about these rewards of regular physical activity either:

- Lower blood pressure and cholesterol levels
- Reduced risk of heart disease, diabetes, osteoporosis, and some cancers
- Better sleep. You'll fall asleep more quickly and sleep more soundly. (Just don't do vigorous exercise right before bedtime, as you need time to wind down.)
- More energy. "Get the blood flowing" is not just an idle saying. Activity brings more oxygen to your tissues. Your heart and lungs work more efficiently.
- Reduced risk of dementia. Increased blood flow helps the brain too.

80 percent of older Americans have at least one chronic condition and 50 percent have at least two.

- Feel happier. Exercise releases chemicals called endorphins that act similarly to morphine in your brain. They reduce pain perception and lead to a feeling of well-being. Avid exercisers will tell you that they can feel the endorphins "kicking in" when they're working out.
- Weight control. Well, this one you already knew. But it is an important consideration. Activity burns calories, helping you to lose—or at least not gain—weight.

How to Turn Back the Clock

If you've been a couch potato for much of the last several decades, you can still enjoy the health benefits of regular exercise. When it comes to physical activity, it turns out it's never too late to start.

Several studies have demonstrated that strength training builds bone and muscle, even in the most elderly, and that it significantly improves mobility and function. In several Tufts University studies, elderly nursing home residents, some as old as 96, increased their strength substantially after just a 10-week strength-training program. Bone density improved and so did balance—so the participants were steadier on their feet and less likely to suffer falls and debilitating fractures.

Another Tufts University study of elderly women found that those who participated in a strength-training program for one year reversed some aspects of aging by 15 to 20 years. Not only did the women increase their bone mass and muscle strength, they became more active in general because they had more energy and self-confidence. Some tried out new activities, such as dancing, bicycling, and roller skating!

Lifting weights can also give your brain a boost. Women who partici-

Men who exercise regularly can gain about two hours of life expectancy for every hour of exercise, according to the Harvard Alumni Study. Regular physical activity appears to reduce the mortality rate by more than a quarter and to increase life expectancy by more than two years when compared to a sedentary population's average, according to a review of the data by the Office of Disease Prevention and Health Promotion in the U.S. Department of Health.

> **IT'S A FACT!**
>
> Everyone talks about how important it is to strengthen your core. But what is a core anyway? The core includes all the muscles that keep your midsection (spine and abdomen) strong and stable. It includes your abdominals, as well as large and small hip and spine muscles. A strong core provides stability and helps you maintain good posture, and it helps prevent low back pain and injury.

pated in a yearlong weight-training study at the University of British Columbia had significantly improved scores in what are known as "executive functions"—skills such as decision-making and conflict resolution. Their scores went up 12.6 percent. They were also able to increase their walking speed, which is often used as a barometer of general health in the elderly.

The Three Legs of Exercise

For the most health benefits, include all three types of exercise: strength training, stretching, and aerobic.

- Strength. Build your muscles, and they will be there for you when you need them: when you lose your balance and need to pull yourself back quickly, when you need to move a chair from one room to another, when you need to carry a bag of groceries or pick up your grandchild.

- Stretch. Stretching improves range of motion, helps prevent injuries, increases flexibility, and helps you warm up before or cool down after a workout.

- Cardio/aerobic. Be good to your heart and lungs. When you're moving rapidly and getting your heart rate up, you're getting more oxygen to your tissues. It strengthens your heart, clears your arteries, and builds endurance. And you're also burning calories. Examples of aerobic exercise: walking, swimming, dancing, and biking.

Location, Location, Location

Let's face it: Starting and sticking with regular exercise is not easy. But you will be more likely to make exercise a habit if you find the right fit.

To do that, you need to ask yourself several questions.

■ Do you like the structure of group classes at a health club or gym? Or is it more helpful when a couple of your friends knock on the door and say, "Let's go walking"?

■ Learn what's out there. Spend time with your pals who are already into fitness. Find out what they like to do, and see if you can tag along.

■ Try as many types of exercise as you can. Many spots that offer classes will let you try one for free before you have to get out your checkbook.

Whether you exercise at home or in a health club, working with a personal trainer can enhance your workout routine. A good source for finding a trainer is the American Council on Exercise at www.acefitness.com. The ACE certifies personal trainers and group exercise instructors. It also trains advanced health and fitness specialists who are experts in prevention and rehabilitation. You'll also find an exercise library, healthy recipes, and equipment reviews on the website.

Location options

■ The comfort of your own home. No parking, no commute, no monthly fees. Just clear a space to move around and stretch, build your strength, and increase your heart rate. To inspire and guide your workout, try exercise videos.

■ Neighborhood. Here's where friends or a high-energy dog can be great companions. Walk around your neighborhood, as fast as you can. Build up your endurance, and stay in touch with what's going on around you. You'll be surprised how friendly your neighbors are.

■ Senior center. Most senior centers offer classes geared to people over 55. The benefit is that you can pay a modest price per class; you don't have to commit to monthly fees.

■ Health club. A health club offers other advantages. You'll find a range of classes offered throughout the day, specialized equipment and trainers, even a pool if you're a swimmer.

■ Gym. When you're looking into joining a gym, make sure it's senior friendly. Do the treadmills start slowly, at a half-mile-per-hour pace? Is there a screening and assessment process for qualities such as balance or osteoporosis? Are there programs available that meet the needs of people with chronic conditions such as cardiovascular disease, balance issues, and muscular weakness?

Cheap, Easy, and Fun Home Fitness Gear

Many people have put themselves on a successful fitness program without ever walking out the front door—except, perhaps, to shop for videos, hand weights, and a floor mat.

All about videos

Here's why you may love videos as a tool for keeping fit:

■ Convenience. They save time, and you can work out at any time of day or night. You don't have to pack a gym bag, drive or park. Just pop a video in the TV and get started.

■ You're in control. You can stop and start videos over and over again to check positions or get a move right.

■ Work out with the pros. Some of the best fitness experts make videos, so you can enjoy their know-how right at home.

■ You never have to get bored. Switch between videos to keep your attention and interest. You can get every level of fitness and every type of exercise just by shopping around.

Ever shop at the thrift store? There you'll likely find lots of exercise videos to choose from for about $1 each. Think of all the folks who have given up on their exercise programs! Their loss is your gain.

■ It's easy to measure your results. When the routine gets easier, you'll know you're making progress.

■ Privacy. Only you will know how you look when you're working out.

The local library should also have exercise videos to borrow or rent. That way you can try many different kinds without having to buy any. Another great source of videos is Collage Video at www.collagevideo.com. You can search for videos based on fitness level, type of exercise, favorite instructor, and kinds of equipment used. Then, you can watch a clip. Return the video, even opened, if you're not happy. And don't forget to read the success stories! They're inspiring.

Hand weights

Hand weights, also called dumbbells, give you an extra boost in strength building. If you're just starting out, begin with a pair of one- or two-pound weights for about $5. You'll find lots of shapes and sizes to pick from. You can also make your own with a 1 pound bag of beans or rice in a sock or a 1 pound can of soup or veggies.

> **IT'S A FACT!**
>
> Sometimes you'll see fast walkers swinging their arms while holding weights. Many experts advise against that because it puts a strain on the wrong part of the arm.

When you work with the weights, you'll do a certain number of repetitions. You can build your strength by slowly increasing the weight and/or the number of repetitions.

Exercise mat

If you're going to exercise on the floor, consider getting a special mat. You could use an old beach towel, but those can slip. You'll find "sticky" mats for yoga, padded with foam if you want something extra soft, or quilted cotton. Whatever you choose, using it will become a positive part of your routine.

Music

You know this instinctively, but recent research has shown that exercising to music increases your rate of respiration, your heart rate, and the intensity and duration of your efforts. And listening to music ehances your enjoyment of physical activity.

The Secret to Staying Mentally Sharp

Forgetfulness comes with getting older—it's something that every person over 50 will ruefully acknowledge. But you don't have to accept mental flabbiness. Take charge of your mental fitness just as you do your physical fitness. Here's how to sharpen your brain so you'll remember your next-door-neighbor's husband's name the next time you see him!

Puzzles and games

Do you like puzzles and games? How about Sudoku or crossword puzzles? Any game or puzzle that challenges you is a terrific mental workout because it requires focused attention, mental flexibility, and problem-solving skills. You'll increase your brain power even if you don't finish them.

At home by yourself? Do

- crossword puzzles, Sudoku, and brain teasers that can be found in your newspaper, in a puzzle book or magazine, or on the Internet.
- a jigsaw puzzle, and gradually challenge yourself with puzzles with more pieces or with fewer visual clues.

Socialize with other people and play

- board games like checkers or Scrabble.
- card games such as bridge or poker.

Go online:

- The Internet opens the door to thousands of free games like Solitaire, Zuma, and video games.
- Search for games that you don't already know about, and try your hand at them.

More ways to increase mental fitness

■ Take a different route to the store. Maybe it will even get you there faster.

■ Switch to your nondominant hand for the computer mouse or while writing a grocery list.

■ Take up crafts such as knitting, painting, woodworking, or making models.

■ Learn—or relearn—a musical instrument.

■ Surf the Internet. Research shows that searching around on the Internet activates different parts of your brain while you are thinking about what to search for next.

■ Brush up on a foreign language or take up a new one.

■ Just play around. You'll come across all kinds of websites that will peak your interest.

SENIOR SECRET

Stay physically fit

Not only does exercise keep your body healthy, it helps your mind too. A group of older adults with memory problems were given a memory test and then asked to exercise three times a week for 50 minutes each time. They did this for six months and then were given a memory test again. The results were clear. Memories improved and stayed better for at least 12 months after the study ended.

This might seem spooky, but exercise actually makes your brain get bigger. A group of seniors had their brains measured, then they exercised by walking regularly for three months. When their brains were measured the second time, they had actually increased in size.

Light Bulb Moment, Seniors!

Are you trying to figure something out? To come up with a brilliant idea, just let it happen. Let your unconscious mind do the work while you're concentrating on routine stuff like washing the dishes, grocery shopping, or mowing the lawn.

When you're concentrating hard to solve a particular problem, the analytical part of your brain (prefrontal lateral area, if you really want to know) is activated. But the creative part of your brain is located elsewhere, in the medial area.

To get the best ideas, you need to activate both the analytical side and the creative side and get them working together. You can't just command your brain to come up with an idea. The way to do that is to relax and let your mind wander.

That's worth repeating: Relax. That's when some of the best ideas are born.

Leave It to the Seniors!

Here's another good reason to enjoy the senior moment. At Stanford University, a team tracked a group of Americans over a 12-year period. They found that as men and women get older, they become more emotionally balanced. They are able to solve highly emotional problems better than younger people. And they get along better with more people.

In fact, seniors "care more and are more compassionate about problems, and that may lead to a more stable world," according to the study's lead author.

6 Staying Connected

What does playing bingo have to do with staying healthy? It's not the temporary increase in heart rate when you jump up to shout "bingo!" And it's not the money you may take home after an evening of card games, either. It's the social aspect of game playing that is good for you. Staying socially connected and engaged turns out to be an elixir of life.

With a Little Help from Friends

Being active and involved feels good, but it's more than a mood booster—not that there's anything wrong with that! Getting out there and doing things actually helps protect you from the kind of physical problems that can decrease your independence. Recent research shows that seniors who ate at restaurants occasionally, traveled (day trips or longer), participated in community groups, went to sports events or religious services, and visited friends were the least likely to be disabled later in life.

SENIOR SECRET

Spending time online is good for your mental health. It reduces depression in seniors by 20 percent or more. Internet use appears to be a low-cost way to expand social interactions, reduce loneliness, and get health information and treatment, according to a 2009 study by the Phoenix Center.

In fact, socially active people were twice as likely as those who are not very active to be disability-free as they aged. They were better at taking care of themselves and were more physically mobile.

Whether you see yourself as an outgoing person or are more the quiet type, your connections with family and friends are precious—and not just because they make you happier and more contented. Your social connections help keep you mentally sharp and physically healthy.

Connecting Via the World Wide Web

Are you wired? That's the term used to describe people who take advantage of the Internet.

The computer and other new technology keep you connected with family, friends, and community resources in very important ways:

> **IT'S A FACT!**
>
> The top four online activities for people over age 60 are Google, Facebook, Yahoo, and YouTube, according to AARP.

■ E-mail lets you write to and receive messages from those near and dear to you quickly—and even in real time if you use an instant-messaging feature.

■ E-mail also lets you receive and send photographs. There's no waiting for the kids to get photos printed and mailed—which could be never! Is your granddaughter pregnant? You can follow the expansion of her belly with the frequent photographs she e-mails to you.

■ Free computer-to-computer long-distance phone services like Skype not only let you talk to people via the Internet, they let you see those people too! If, like increasing numbers of grandparents, you live some distance from your grandchildren, you can visit with them every day if you want via Skype. Even if the children and grandchildren lived closer, you might not see them in person as often as you are able to visit with them virtually.

■ Some of the latest cell phones have video-chatting and video-conferencing capabilities. That means you can be in touch with friends and family wherever they (or you) roam.

■ Facebook lets you keep up to date with family members unobtrusively—and there's an immediacy to it that is hard to duplicate. It turns out to be an especially valuable way to connect with and even become close with the grandkids. If they accept you as a friend on Facebook—which many will do even if they don't "friend" their own parents—you can follow their daily (sometimes hourly!) postings and status updates, see their most recent photographs, and get a sense of their lives and what's on their minds.

Getting Technical

If you haven't already joined the Internet generation or your skills aren't up to snuff, there are lots of places to get help learning the ropes. Here are some to get you started:

■ Ask a friend or relative (especially grandchildren—it's another opportunity for bonding!) who is computer savvy to teach you.

■ Take a free or low-cost computer class locally. Libraries, community colleges, park districts, community centers, senior centers, and local government offices (such as cities or suburbs, townships, and counties) often offer beginning computer classes for older adults. Check them all out to find the least expensive, most convenient classes.

IT'S A FACT!

Seniors age 65 and older trail the national average in using the World Wide Web. Nearly half (48 percent) of senior citizens are Internet users, but only 35 percent have access at home, according to a 2009 FCC survey.

- If you don't own a computer, you will find free computers to use at libraries and at senior or community centers.

- Contact your local Area Agency on Aging. You can call the Eldercare Locator at 800–677–1116 or visit www.eldercare.gov.

- Check into Generations on Line, a digital inclusion initiative of Senior Service America. This is an online computer tutorial, with peer coaches, designed for low-income older adult learners. It is available through local partners at more than 300 sites throughout the United States, including rural areas. For more information, visit www.seniorserviceamerica.org and click on the Digital Inclusion Initiative tab at the top of the page. You can find local partners in your state. To reach GOL by phone, call 301–578–8900.

E-mail Etiquette and Protection

Where's Amy Vanderbilt when you need her? New rules of etiquette have developed for writing and sending e-mail messages, and there are also some important safety rules. These are some basics so you don't inadvertently send the wrong message or leave yourself vulnerable to cyber attacks.

- Do not write in all capital letters. This is considered akin to shouting or yelling at the recipient. (DO NOT USE

ALL CAPS—see, doesn't that feel like the letters are screaming at you?).

■ If you're sending an e-mail to many people, not just to a small circle of friends or relatives who know each other, list all the e-mail addresses in the BCC (Blind Carbon Copy) field instead of in the To or CC field. That way you are not sharing everyone's e-mail addresses with strangers.

■ Log out of your e-mail account when you are not using it. This is especially important if you are using a public computer, such as those at a library, community center, or even a store. Your e-mail is protected by a password, but if you don't sign out, anyone who uses the computer next could access your e-mail—putting you at risk for identity theft and all kinds of mischief using your personal information.

■ Do not accept your computer's invitation, via a pop-up message, to "remember your password." You may be prompted frequently to do that, but although it may seem convenient, it is actually quite dangerous. If the computer

Scam Alert!

What will the scammers think of next? Con artists are now calling seniors claiming to be a grandchild in need. They say they're traveling and need $500 sent by way of Western Union right away. If this happens to you, do these things before you panic and send cash:

■ Check with the parents, even if the "grandkid" said to keep it a secret.

■ Ask personal questions that only the real grandchild would know how to answer.

■ Call the police.

remembers your password for you, then anyone who opens it has access to your e-mail—and through it to other personal information.

Friends Indeed

Want to predict how you'll feel after you retire? Count the number of friends you have, not how much money you squirreled away or how healthy you are.

That's right: The most powerful predictor of post-retirement happiness is the size of your social network, says a University of Michigan study. The researchers could even give the happiness factor a number: 16. Study participants who said they were "most satisfied" with life had an average of 16 people in their social networks. Those who were least satisfied had networks of fewer than 10 people.

> **IT'S A FACT!**
>
> Half of Internet users ages 50 to 64 and 26 percent of users age 65 and older use social networking sites.

The results stand to reason, since retirement can shrink the amount of daily interaction you have with people and leave you feeling isolated. Having a solid group of good friends will provide the emotional support you need to negotiate the life changes that come with retirement. Even if you're ecstatic about retirement, it is still a significant life event—and positive changes cause stress, too, as you adjust to the new normal.

Friendship Silver and Gold

Friends understand your life in a way that family does not. And they can be a buffer when family troubles create tough times. Most of all, friends are fun.

What to do if you come up several friends short of the magic number in your social network?

■ Be a good friend—to those you already have and to acquaintances you may not have put yourself out for before. Strengthen all the relationships you have.

■ Be on the lookout. Join clubs and organizations or participate in activities and events in which you are interested. Keep your eyes open for someone interesting to talk with who shares your passions.

■ Reconnect with old friends. Everyone loses touch with old friends over the years while working and raising families, so don't let embarrassment get in your way. This is the perfect time to get reacquainted—and to reminisce. Even if a significant number of years have passed, old friends will feel comfortable immediately.

■ Start using social networking tools like Facebook and Twitter. These will take you in directions that you may not be able to imagine. From finding former schoolmates to meeting people with similar health issues, social networking sites have the capacity to expand your universe exponentially.

Find an interest group for older adults nearby by checking out www.seniors.meetup.com. Meetup.com is a huge network of local groups. It provides the platform for people to organize and meet with like-minded folks. You can join a group that's already been formed, or you can create your own.

- Make friends with people who are younger than you are. Younger friends can bring energy to your life and fill in the holes left by friends who are absent due to moves, illness, or even death.

Dating and Romance

If you're a single senior, you've got plenty of company. According to the U.S. Census Bureau, about 46 percent of Americans older than age 65 do not have a partner. Millions of older Americans are widowed, divorced, or separated, or were never married.

Some seniors are quite happy to be on their own, but many are looking for someone with whom to share and enjoy life. Companionship is a priority. Love and romance would be great, of course, though not all seniors are necessarily interested in marriage. Whatever your desires and dreams, it takes some effort to seek and find a person you can care about and who cares for you.

Ready or not?

Before you put a toe in the dating waters, though, be sure you're ready.

IT'S A FACT!

Social networking by people age 50 and older increased from 22 percent to 42 percent, almost doubling from 2009 to 2010. What are they doing online? Staying in touch with friends, family, and colleagues by sharing links, photos, and videos; keeping up with the news; and writing and reading status updates with a growing network of contacts, according to the Pew Research Center's report on Older Adults and Social Media.

If you have lost a partner through death or divorce, ask your-self a few questions before jumping into the dating game:

■ Are you past the emotions of the previous relationship?

■ Do you feel you have to tell your life story on the first date?

■ Are you ready to listen to the other person?

■ Are you ready to have fun?

One dating expert suggests that you make a short list of what you are looking for in a partner. There is a good chance you're looking for different traits than you wanted when you were dating in your teens and twenties.

Online Dating

It's not easy for seniors to meet someone to date or to find a potential new partner. That's why many are taking their cues from younger singles and trying their luck on the Internet. Some of the popular sites are www.seniors.com, www.match.com, and www.eharmony.com. There's also a dating site just for people over 50 called OurTime.com.

When you go online, you might be able to browse the prospects a bit without signing up, but at some point early on, you will be asked to fill out a personal profile before you will be allowed access to more. And sooner or later you'll need to pay a fee, as these sites all charge for continued access and usage. If you do sign up, you'll want to include a picture, so start looking for one that puts your best face forward. Or ask a friend to take a new photo of you to post. One expert suggests taking a picture of yourself doing something you enjoy.

Once you find someone who looks interesting, get acquainted first by e-mail and then by phone. When you're ready to meet in person, choose a public place, such as a coffee shop or restaurant.

For your protection

Remember, there are charmers out there who are looking to rip you off. Until you know your new love really, really well, be cautious.

■ Make the first dates in the daytime and for short amounts of time—just for coffee, for example.

■ Don't give out your home phone number or your home address. This allows you to guard your personal information until you get to know the person well.

■ When you're going to meet someone, always let friends or family know where you are going and when.

IT'S A FACT!

Be careful out there! Sexually transmitted diseases (STDs) are on the rise among American seniors. Nationally, the incidence of chlamydia and syphilis among those age 55 and older rose 43 percent between 2005 and 2009, according to the Centers for Disease Control and Prevention. In South Florida, perhaps the senior capitol of the United States, there was a 60 percent rise in the incidence of those diseases.

The reason for this dramatic increase? Experts attribute it to more socialization among seniors because of the growing numbers of retirement communities, increased dating activity due to Internet contacts, the availability of medications like Viagra and Cialis that treat erectile dysfunction, infrequent use of condoms, and the increased longevity and good health of older adults.

- Watch out for anyone who might want to borrow money or get information about your bank account.

- Do not leave your purse or wallet open or unattended.

- Don't drink alcohol. It may relax you, but it will also cloud your judgment and relax your inhibitions. You want to be clear-headed and in control on the first several dates at least.

- Keep your drink, no matter what kind it is, near you, and don't leave it unguarded to avoid tampering.

Pet Power

Do you share your home with a special animal? If a pet is part of your life, then you are taking care of more than a Fido or Fluffy. You are taking care of yourself!

Research shows that pets help people live longer and better lives. Pet owners get over illnesses more quickly and have lower blood pressure and cholesterol levels than nonowners, and they need to visit the doctor less frequently.

If you are thinking of getting a pet, make sure it fits your lifestyle. This is not the time to take on a big, strong, demanding animal. Instead consider adopting a mature cat or dog who is past the rambunctious stage and won't take over your home.

If you can't adopt a pet, you can get your strokes in and reap the health benefits by volunteering at a local animal shelter. Grooming, petting, and playing with furry friends are therapeutic activities, even if the pets aren't yours.

If your dog needs and loves a walk, then you have a built-in reminder to get out and exercise. Once you're out, you might chat with another dog owner, take in a sunny day, and generally clear your head. All the while, you're getting that extra 20 to 30 minutes of physical activity that keeps you healthy.

Your dog or cat loves you for yourself, not because you're wearing the latest fashion. A pet's unconditional love is a powerful antidepressant. If petting your dog or cat makes you feel good, it's not an accident. It's scientific. Cuddling with your four-legged pal releases endorphins, hormones that help you relax.

So who cares if there's a little pet hair sticking to your nice black slacks?

Building Community

We are part of many different kinds of communities during our lives, but where we live is the most obvious and has the most impact. As we get older our communities change, and so do our needs and desires. We leave some communities, such as our workplace, and need to build connections to new ones. People who feel connected are happier and healthier.

New housing options

It used to be that senior citizens only had a few options when it came to housing: living independently in a home or apartment, or moving to an assisted living or nursing home situation that felt more like a human warehouse than a home or community.

Today, there are many more possibilities. A whole spectrum of housing options have been developed—and more continue to be developed—so that you truly can pick a living arrangement that fits your personality, your budget, and your needs and also fosters the connections that are so critical to your long-term health and satisfaction.

Here are some newer living options to consider that you may not know about:

COHOUSING In cohousing communities, residents may have the best of both worlds: independence and strong community life. Residents live independently, usually in a single-family detached home, a townhome, or a condo apartment, but share common spaces that encourage social contact. There is a common house that functions as a social center and includes a dining room and kitchen for optional group meals several times a week, recreational spaces, and other amenities. Decisions about allocation of dues are made together as a community, and residents meet regularly to socialize, to solve problems, and to develop

SENIOR SECRET

The *Chicago Tribune* took a list of U.S. cities with the most single people over age 65 and crossed it with their Best Places to Retire search tool to offer up the best spots in the country to retire for older adults who are looking to meet fun-loving age-mates.

This is the top-ten list that resulted:

- Columbus, Georgia
- Fort Lauderdale, Florida
- Memphis, Tennessee
- Milford, Connecticut
- Providence, Rhode Island
- Quincy, Massachusetts
- Reno, Nevada
- Santa Fe, New Mexico
- Santa Rosa, California
- Towson, Maryland

community policies. Cohousing communities are sometimes designed with input from future residents, and the homes are clustered to promote contact with neighbors and for proximity to the common house.

For more information about cohousing, contact the Cohousing Association of the United States at 812–618–2646 or www.cohousing.org. (You can write to the organization at P.O. Box 28218, Seattle Washington, 98118.)

VILLAGES This new type of community helps older people with the low-cost support they need to stay in their own homes. It's an "aging in place" model, which many seniors prefer. The first village started in Boston in 2001, and now there are at least 56 villages in the United States—with more than 120 in the works.

Money-Rates.com has put together a list of the best states in which to retire—and the list may surprise you. A number of different factors were considered, including climate, crime rate, life expectancy, cost of living, job opportunities, and taxes, in deciding on the final list. Here it is. Let's hope your kids and grandkids live in some of them!

Best-rated States for Retirement

1. New Hampshire	**6.** Virginia
2. Hawaii	**7.** Utah
3. South Dakota	**8.** Connecticut
4. North Dakota	**9.** Vermont
5. Iowa	**10.** Idaho

Here's how it works: Members pay a reasonable yearly fee, which entitles them to services that run the gamut from home repairs to transportation to health and wellness programs to social and educational activities. Villages are run by volunteers and paid staff.

For more information, contact Village to Village Network at 617–299–9NET or visit www.vtvnetwork.org.

CONTINUING CARE RETIREMENT COMMUNITIES WITHOUT WALLS

The standard continuing care retirement community (CCRC) offers different levels of health care on one campus, so you can obtain increasing amounts of assistance as you need it without having to move to a new community or residence. Generally there is a one-time entrance fee and then monthly premiums for a wide range of other services, such as nursing care, housekeeping, meals, and social programming.

A newer version of a CCRC is the Continuing Care at Home (CCAH) program, which is a more affordable alternative that allows you to remain in your own home while receiving services such as care coordination and routine home maintenance, in-home caregivers, transportation, meals, and wellness programs. With a CCAH, you can develop your own personalized care plan. CCAH programs are sometimes operated by nonprofit organizations. To find information about CCAHs in your area, contact your local or state's department of aging.

SHARED HOUSING This is another creative way to remain in your home, lower your costs, and have a source of companionship. You share your home with an unrelated person who needs a place to live. There are many match-up programs across the country; some only function as referral services while others offer matching services and follow-up throughout the homesharing relationship.

The National Shared Housing Resource Center, founded by Gray Panther activist Maggie Kuhn in 1981, is an information clearinghouse on shared housing. On its website, www.nationalsharedhousing.org, you'll find a list of regional representatives to contact for help locating a shared housing matching service in your area.

Adapting Your Home

Aging in place is a great idea, but what if your current residence isn't so user-friendly as you get older? An industry has sprung up with specialists trained to help people age 50 and older alter their homes to meet their changing needs.

The Certified Aging in Place Specialist is a designation developed by the National Association of Home Builders Remodelers Council, in collaboration with AARP, the NAHB Research Center, and the NAHB Seniors Housing Council, to give professionals the skills they need to serve the older adult population. Certified aging-in-place specialists (CAPS) are trained to modify homes and provide solutions to common problems that seniors confront in their daily lives. These changes can be as simple as adding grab bars to the shower or tub area and lever door handles in place of knobs to make them easier to open. Other common remodeling improvements are widening doorways to accommodate a wheelchair and installing elevated sinks and dishwashers to reduce bending and back strain.

For more information and to find CAPS in your area, visit the AARP website and search for "CAPS locator."

7 Senior Fun, On the Road and At Home

If you've put off traveling, starting a hobby, or doing volunteer work, now's the time to fulfill those yearnings. We'll help you turn your dreams into reality. And if you're looking for some new ideas, you'll find those here too.

Travel Ideas—where to go and ways to get there

Being a senior gives you the flexibility and freedom to travel throughout the year, not just at major holidays or vacation times. That makes traveling more cost-effective and more pleasant, since you can avoid peak travel times. On top of that, seniors almost always get discounts on hotels, car rentals, entertainment, and more. For more discounts, see Chapter 8.

Whether your idea of a great trip is packing up the car for a road trip or flying to some distant location, now's the time to get out of town!

Where to go? Here are some possibilities.

National Parks

As a senior aged 62 or older, you get special treatment at national parks and recreation areas with an America the Beautiful–The National Parks and Federal Recreational Lands Senior Pass. It costs only $10—for your lifetime! In fact, you can bring your family or friends (up to three adults who are traveling with you in a noncommercial vehicle;

children under 16 are always admitted free). The Senior Pass admits you to more than 2,000 recreation sites around the country and comes with a 50-percent discount on some amenities such as camping and swimming.

Where do I sign up, you say? You can buy the America the Beautiful Senior Pass in person at a participating federal recreation site or office. You'll need to show proof of your age and citizenship or permanent resident status. You can also purchase the pass by mail, but it will cost you an extra 10 bucks for processing. Go to http://store.usgs.gov/pass/index.html and click on "Senior Pass" in the right-hand column for more information on the pass and a link to the application by mail.

To find out more about a specific park or site, such as what the facilities are, whether you need reservations, the condition and length of hiking and biking trails, and more, start with the website www.nps.gov or call 202–208–3100.

One of the most popular park service sites is Gettysburg National Military Park in Pennsylvania, where a bloody three-day battle turned the tide of the Civil War. You can take a bus tour or a self-guided tape tour of the battlefield, but you can also try a tour that is unique to Gettysburg. Specially trained Licensed Battlefield Guides will ride in your car with you as you drive the battlefield, offering information and answering questions for just you and your companions. This guide service has roots that go back to 1863, right after the battle, when local residents would informally take visitors around to explain what had happened. Cost is $50 for up to six people in a vehicle.

Trading places

If your travel bug is thwarted by the high cost of hotels or rentals, consider exchanging homes with a senior in another part of the country—or another country altogether. You'll get all the comforts of a real home, save on meals, and may even get the use of a car, all without draining your bank account.

To see the array of places you can go, check out Seniors Home Exchange at www.seniorshomeexchange.com. Options include a straight exchange (you go to their place, they go to yours) or a hospitality visit (you visit them, then they visit you). There are other home exchange programs, but Seniors Home Exchange is specifically for those over age 50.

The cost to list your home and search for a trade is $79 for three years. Nontraditional homes such as motor homes are also listed, as well as some rentals that don't involve a swap.

Tour companies specializing in seniors

One of the pleasures of taking a tour is meeting and getting to know new people. If you book your tour through a company that specializes in senior

SENIOR SECRET

There are a ton of travel discounts and perks available to seniors, but they're not always advertised or offered. You have to speak up and ask in order to find out about many of them. So don't hesitate to identify yourself as a senior and find out if there are any deals for you. Ask and you shall receive!

At the same time, though, also inquire about other discounts available. The senior discount is not always the deepest one—there may be a better deal or a lower rate.

travel, chances are good that your traveling companions will share your interests and understand the quirks of being over 50. Tours for seniors are more tuned in to accommodating the unique needs of older adults.

The following are tours approved by and affiliated with AARP. With each one, you'll get a small gift or discount when you sign up.

ROAD SCHOLAR Travel and learn about your destination by going on a trip with Road Scholar (formerly called Elder-hostel). Designed for adults over 50, Road Scholar offers more than 7,000 educational travel experiences in the United States and 150 countries. Expert instructors, authorities in their subjects, bring topics alive, but learning is also experiential. Travelers stay in many types of accommodations, including B&Bs, hotels, and inns.

Tours are designed to be affordable and almost always are all-inclusive. You won't run into "extras" that will drive up the cost of the trip. The cost also includes the Travel Assistance Plan to make sure you will be taken care of in case of a medical emergency.

Road Scholar provides detailed information about the level of physical activity that will be needed on any given trip. So, if you have any kind of limitation or disability, you can select a trip that will allow you to participate to the max.

Road Scholar trips are single-friendly and considered to be warm and inclusive. People without partners are comfortable and can choose to room alone or be matched with a roommate.

Explore your options at www.roadscholar.org or call 1–800–454–5768 Monday–Saturday to have a catalog mailed to you.

GRAND CIRCLE TOURS Grand Circle Tours was founded in 1958 by Ethel Andrus, the retired teacher who also founded AARP. She wanted seniors to have an opportunity to discover local people and cultures on trips marked by high standards of service and a relaxed pace. Grand Circle's literature describes the amount of walking in each tour, and you can check with the company for more details.

Tours spend two or three nights in each city (or longer in the Super Leisure category) to set a more leisurely pace than is typical of tours. Headsets are provided so you can clearly hear the trip leader even in noisy environments. And the company offers an unconditional price guarantee, allowing you to cancel at any time up to the day of departure and retain the full value of your trip, so you can plan with confidence.

Only a few Grand Circle tours are in the United States or North America. Most will take you to more exotic locations—Africa, Asia, Europe, the Middle East, the South Pacific, and South America.

For more information, contact Grand Circle Tours at www.gct.com or call 800–959–0405.

> **SENIOR SECRET**
>
> When you're a senior and your companion or visitors are not, they may still be able to get in on your senior rate. Oftentimes only the person buying tickets or booking a trip is required to meet the age requirement. Always check to see if your senior rate applies to everyone in your party (or just your significant other) regardless of their age. Assuming that it doesn't can cost you—or them—dearly.

COLLETTE VACATIONS Another educational touring option is Collette Vacations. Although not strictly for seniors, Collette's Smithsonian Journeys Travel Adventures offer a learning experience with local experts and value pricing.

Tours in North and South America, Europe, and Asia are available. Go to www.collettevacations.com or call 800–437–0241 for information.

GRAND EUROPEAN TOURS The company claims it offers the world's most leisurely tours. Here are features that are attractive to seniors:

- A knowledgeable tour leader as well as local guides who share their first-hand knowledge and experience. Personal audio systems are available.
- Meals that feature local cuisine, as well as opportunities to pick from a list of other restaurants without additional cost.
- Special opportunities to experience a new culture— perhaps you will enjoy a meal in a local family's home or attend a local cultural event.

Grand European does not just offer tours to Europe. It has tours to the Middle East, North and South America, New Zealand, and Australia. Information is at www.getours.com or call 877–622–9109.

YMT VACATIONS YMT offers senior-friendly tours that combine good value with more than 40 years of experience. The company offers land tours with motor coaches and land/cruise combinations to a few destinations in the Americas, Europe, and the Middle East.

In the U.S., you might try the Southwestern Tour and Balloon Fiesta. On that tour, you'll go to the international hot air balloon festival in Albuquerque, then continue on to visit

Scam Alert!

Seniors are the favorite target of travel scammers. They'll come after you on the telephone, over the internet, and through the mail, offering free trips and incredible discounts that sound like a dream come true. Instead, these will turn into a nightmare if you fall for them.

Follow this advice to avoid losing your hard-earned money or going on a vacation that isn't.

- Never accept an offer that requires you to give your credit card number or bank account information over the phone.
- Refuse "free" vacations for which you only have to pay "handling" or other fees.
- Don't wire money or send it by messenger.
- Always ask for written information that details everything that's included and any additional costs.
- Don't take out a membership or send a deposit in order to qualify for a discounted or free trip.
- Always check the reputation of the company. Contacting the Better Business Bureau is a great place to start.
- File a report with the Federal Trade Commission, 877-FTC-HELP (1-877-382-4357), if you think you have been scammed.

Santa Fe, the Petrified Forest, the red rocks of Sedona, and White Sands National Monument. Or head to the ancient land of Egypt where you'll visit the pyramids at Giza and take a four-day cruise down the Nile, stopping at ancient temples along the way.

To find out more, check www.ymtvacations.com or call 800–922–9000.

Cruising for fun

Many travelers take cruises because they're a good value. The cruise covers room and board, so your expenses are predictable, and there is a lot to do on the ship. If you'd like to take a cruise, here are a few tips:

■ Don't hesitate to use a travel agent to research and book your cruise. Travel agents know the territory, and because they have close ties to the cruise lines, they just might come up with upgrades and other perks.

■ You are usually better off booking your own flights, rather than arranging them with the cruise line (although there are exceptions). Just be sure to allow plenty of time so the ship doesn't leave without you! Experts suggest that you arrive in the departure city a day ahead.

■ Tipping is less complicated than it used to be, since ships now charge a set amount per day to cover restaurant servers and your cabin steward. Of course you're welcome to tip extra if you receive exceptional service. When you buy drinks, a gratuity of 15 to 18 percent is automatically added.

TOP SECRET ★ TOP SECRET ★ TOP SECRET ★ TOP SECRET

SENIOR SECRET

Enjoy the luxury of a four-star hotel for under $50. Eat lunch or have a drink at a top-rated hotel to celebrate a special occasion or just to feel extravagant on a budget. If you want a more special experience, go for high tea. It will cost you more but is quite fun.

THE AARP TRAVEL CENTER AARP members can take advantage of multiple discounts on all kinds of travel and travel-associated activities. The AARP Travel Center is powered by Expedia and combines members-only discounts with exclusive travel deals from Expedia. You can save on hotels, flights, cruises, cars, and vacation packages. You'll also get additional member benefits such as no booking fees on flights or cruises and up to 25 percent off AARP-preferred car rental companies. Go to http://www.aarp.org/benefits-discounts/travel-discounts/ for more information or call 1-800-675-4318.

> **IT'S A FACT!**
>
> In the 1960s, Arthur Frommer wrote the book on student travel, *Europe on $5 a Day,* which many of a certain age remember well. He is still going strong, with one of the best budget travel websites at www.budgettravelonline.com. Or check out his magazine *Budget Travel*.

Adventures in Volunteering: At Home and Away

One of the most meaningful ways to use your new free time is to volunteer. There are so many opportunities to share and grow your skills, pursue an interest, and/or support a cause—and they're as close as your neighborhood or as distant as a foreign land. No matter what you choose to do or where, you will gain as much as you give.

Your hometown needs you

From A (animal shelters) to Z (the zoo), everywhere you turn, there's a chance to use your skills to make a difference in your own community. Most towns have Girl and Boy Scout chapters; service clubs such as the Elks and Rotary;

libraries; history centers and historic buildings; homeless shelters, hospices, and nursing homes; parks and recreation programs; museums; and local schools—most if not all of which use volunteers in a number of different ways. To find a local agency that helps the elderly, go to this national center's website: www.eldercare.gov or call 800–577–1116.

You can use your talents, counsel, or just read to someone who cannot do it for himself. Teach someone how to read or get started on the computer. Lend a hand to someone who needs child care. Or help someone who is without a home. Deliver Meals on Wheels, or wash dishes or serve meals at a soup kitchen. Support your political values by helping a candidate.

Here are some organized volunteer programs that you may not know about.

UNCLE SAM NEEDS YOU If you want to explore volunteerism with the national government, a good place to begin is www.volunteer.gov/gov. This website combines opportunities from nine federal agencies

SENIOR SECRET ★ TOP SECRET ★

Volunteering is good for your health! Several studies have shown that older adults reap both physical and mental health benefits from participating in volunteer activities. One study found that volunteer work is as beneficial as fitness activities in lowering the risk of death. Another showed that low-income minority seniors who volunteered in public elementary schools outscored their contemporaries who did not volunteer in both physical strength and cognitive ability. Volunteering also has been shown to decrease the risk of depression among those age 65 and older.

including the National Park Service, the U.S. Forest Service, Natural Resources Conservation Service, and the National Oceanic & Atmospheric Administration. A few state agencies are also included.

For instance, if you type "senior" into the search box, you might find that Deer Creek Lake in Sterling, Ohio, would like help building butterfly boxes, monitoring the fish, and helping out in the visitor center or office.

Key points: There is no upper age limit when you volunteer for Uncle Sam. While volunteering, you are covered for any injuries that might happen.

Fido can help too! Animals are therapeutic in ways that humans are not. Research shows that a visit from a therapy dog can lower blood pressure and decrease levels of stress hormones in hospital patients and nursing home residents. One study showed that a visit with a dog before an MRI reduced patient anxiety enough to eliminate the need for anti-anxiety medication. Therapy dogs are used to encourage children to read (they will happily read out loud to a rapt doggie) and people of all ages to speak who are having trouble vocalizing. They have been used to reduce loneliness in nursing home patients and to increase interaction among people with dementia.

If you and your four-footed best friend would like to try out as a therapy team, contact The Delta Society, which is dedicated to helping people by taking advantage of the human-canine bond. Information about training for service and therapy animals is available at www.deltasociety.org and 425–679–5500.

PROTECTING THE ELDERLY Help protect elderly nursing home patients from neglect or abuse by becoming a Long-Term Care Ombudsman (someone who helps resolve problems or complaints). In 2009, more than 11,000 volunteer ombudsmen helped to resolve more than 233,000 complaints.

Go to the Administration on Aging, www.aoa.gov, and search for "elder rights," which will lead you to the Long-Term Care Ombudsman section. Or call the AOA at 800–677–1116. Find out more about what ombudsmen do at the National Long-Term Care Ombudsman Resource Center, www.ltcombudsman.org.

SENIOR CORPS, HELPING SENIORS HELP AMERICA The National Senior Service Corps helps connect people age 55 and older with volunteer opportunities in their communities. It offers several programs:

■ The Foster Grandparent Program, in which seniors provide emotional and/or educational support to children in need. Children might be victims of abuse or handicapped in some way. Volunteers receive training and possibly a modest expense reimbursement.

■ The Senior Companion Program puts seniors together with other adults in their community who have trouble performing everyday activities. Volunteers may assist in shopping, light chores, and doctor visits. Creating friendships and relationships is one of the goals of the program.

■ Retired and Senior Volunteer Program (RSVP) matches a senior's skills and available time with the needs of the local community. The tasks can vary from helping to build a house to immunizing children to helping nonprofit organizations devoted to protecting the environment.

For more info, go to www.seniorcorps.org or 800–424–8867.

CITIZEN CORPS This program was developed after the terrorist attacks on September 11, 2011, to help communities be better prepared to respond—and help first responders to respond—to terrorism, crime, public health issues, and natural disasters. This is accomplished through a national network of state, local, and tribal Citizen Corps Councils.

Volunteers take classes in emergency preparedness and response for their communities and are then able to support professional responders and disaster relief groups if and when they are needed.

Go to www.citizencorps.gov to learn more about Citizen Corps. To find a local council, click on the Citizen Corps Councils tab at the top of the page and select "Find Nearby Council" from the drop-down menu. You can enter your zip code and the number of miles away from home base that you're willing to travel.

> **IT'S A FACT!**
>
> What do seniors say are the most appealing ways to volunteer? The top five in order: working with children, with religious organizations, with other seniors, at a hospital, or helping homeless/poor people.

Citizens Corps is administered by the Federal Emergency Management Agency within Homeland Security.

MORE GOVERNMENT VOLUNTEER OPTIONS Check out these possibilities:

- Peace Corps (currently 5 percent of volunteers are age 50 or older): www.peacecorps.gov or 800-424-8580
- AmeriCorps VISTA: www.americorps.gov/about/programs/vista.asp

- Senior Medicare Patrol: www.smpresource.org or 877-808-2468
- America Reads: www2.ed.gov/americareads or 202-401-8888

Taking on medical problems

If you or a loved one have endured a serious medical condition or illness, chances are there was a group that helped you through it. Pay it forward by volunteering for an illness-specific organization, such as the American Cancer Society, the American Heart Association, the Arthritis Foundation, and the National Multiple Sclerosis Society.

At Your Leisure

Retirement brings more free time, which you can use to pursue an interest that you weren't able to fit into your schedule before. Here are a couple real-life examples to start your creative juices flowing.

Start a new special interest group

If you have a special interest but there is no group in your area to join, start one of your own! For example:

- In Illinois, a woman started a wine-tasting club in her hometown that meets six times a year. She planned it while she was still working but waited until she was retired before getting the group going. Maintaining friendships was as much a goal as learning about wine.
- One man, who had recently retired and moved to North Carolina, wanted to find a group to share his passion for model airplanes that can be flown remotely. He didn't know anyone in his new town, so he posted notices in

free advertising papers. His efforts paid off in a big way. Today there are about 50 members of the model plane club, and they meet every Saturday to fly their planes in an open field.

Uncover and record family history

As the younger generation grows up and older generations fade away, many seniors feel a sense of urgency to understand and record their family history, for themselves and for the younger generation.

PHOTOS Find and make copies of important photographs so that each of your children and other important family members can have their own set. Photos can be shared, unlike Grandma's special vase, which can only go to one person.

The digital age has made photo sharing quick and easy—if you've joined the digital age, that is. If you have stacks of photos that you'd like to scan and put on the computer, enlist a young person to show you how. There are also services that will do it for you—for a fee, of

You have the World War II photo of your dad in a place of honor, but do you know where he served? Or when he was called up and discharged? If you'd like to get the full service record, you can do that as a next of kin (parent, spouse, or child). Records for millions of military personnel are stored at the National Personnel Records Center-Military Personnel Records (NPRC-MPR). There is no cost to request the records if you are the actual military service member or the next of kin. Call 800–234–8861, or check at the website for the Department of Defense, www.defense.gov.

course. You mail the photos and they return the pictures along with CDs. One of the more highly rated is ScanCafe at www.scancafe.com and 866–745–0392. Another option is BritePix at www.britepix.com and 800–795–4574.

Make sure photos have names and dates on the back. At the time they're taken, it's easy to think you'll always remember who that cute little baby is. But 50 years later, no one remembers and the mystery may never be solved.

FAMILY TREE If your relatives immigrated to the United States through Ellis Island, you can search for them via a free online database. Go to www.ellisisland.com. If you want to find out who your ancestors are, a good place to start is www.ancestry.com. Census records, immigration records, and family trees are just a few of the ways you can learn more about where you came from. You'll get a 14-day free trial before you need to sign up as a member.

STORIES When we're young, we think we'll remember family stories forever. When we're older, though, we know they're precious and easily forgotten. If you keep your family history alive, your grandchildren will thank you. Write them all down so they are not lost to future generations. Interview older relatives who are still around, and write down any information or stories they tell you. If you are having a hard time getting started, check with your local community college or senior center. They often sponsor groups that get together regularly to share the writing experience.

You can also interview relatives and make a video of them answering your questions, telling stories, and more. You won't be preserving just their words, you'll be capturing the character of the storyteller and the emotional weight or comic relief of the story.

More ideas

What you do in this phase of life is limited only by your imagination. Here are some quick suggestions to get your own ideas flowing:

■ Learn something new. Most community colleges and universities have classes specifically designed for older adults. Pursue an area of interest, such as British literature or Middle Eastern history, take a language, explore your artistic side with a pottery or painting class, or learn about the latest technology. The options are virtually unlimited. You can take a class in an area of interest or pursue a degree.

Want to attend a play or concert for free? Volunteer to be an usher. It's win-win for you and for the venue.

■ Join a book club. You'll often find these at community centers; churches, synagogues, and other houses of worship; libraries; and bookstores. You can also start your own. Check out Reader's Circle, www.readerscircle.org, a website that lists book clubs all over the country. Just enter your zip code in the search box, and you will receive a list of book clubs near you. You can also use the site to post your own book club.

■ Get physical! Take up a sport, join a bike riding group, do yoga or tai chi, or take a self-defense class. Your local park district is a good place to find these.

■ Start journaling or take a memoir writing class.

■ Go gourmet. Take cooking classes at a local culinary arts school or a kitchen product store.

Challenge Yourself

Do you have a "bucket list"—a list of all the things you want to do, explore, learn, and discover while you still can? If you've been compiling such a list over the years, this is a good time to break it out. If you don't have one, there's no time like the present to make one!

Bucket lists are incredibly inspiring. They turn wishes into reality as you start chipping away at them. They'll help you plan for and look forward to the future.

Some people make their list a personal challenge. Perhaps they want to visit all 50 states or visit all 393 national parks. Either of those challenges will take you far and wide. If something like that is part of your bucket list, pick up a souvenir from each state—a coffee cup, a snow globe, a native rock, a doll—something distinctive for each territory—to trigger good memories when you are home. Watch your collection grow. Be sure to hang a U.S. map on the wall so you can mark your progress.

Bucket lists can contain the simplest desires, like having a hot fudge sundae at that famous ice cream parlor in the next town, to more daredevil adventures like skydiving. They can be limited to things you can do within a certain distance from your home, within a certain budget, or with certain people. It's all up to you.

The wishes you have and the goals you set are deeply personal, and so will your satisfaction be as you enrich your life by following your dreams.

8 Bargains, Discounts, and Freebies

Looking for more ways to save money? After all, you live in the land of the free, home of the bargain seeker. Search out and take advantage of all that's out there—the free/almost-free, coupons, bargains, and discounts. Use your senior status and savvy to snag great deals. You'll enjoy life even more when you're shaving dollars off the price, and you'll hang onto the green stuff in your wallet to put away for savings or to increase your purchasing power.

Coupons: Not Just in Your Sunday Paper

For the traditional coupon-clipper, the Sunday sales fliers still hold a wealth of deals. Groceries, electronics, jewelry, clothing, travel, fine dining, and other industries fill that plastic pouch with deals (much better protected from the elements than the rest of the paper) week in and week out. But is that the only way to save—searching laboriously through the lot for the few deals that apply or appeal to you?

IT'S A FACT!

Coca-Cola issued the first coupon in 1888.

There are many other places to find coupons and discounts, largely on the Internet. And most of these aren't limited to seniors—they're available to everyone! So hook up your computer (or find an obliging grandchild to do it) and check out some of these places for general coupon shopping. Sites specifically for the over-50 crowd can be found a little later in this chapter.

COUPONS.COM The founder of www.coupons.com got the idea for this website when he watched his father-in-law clipping coupons from the Sunday paper. It's now the 43rd-largest website in the United States. Check out the local coupons; you'll most likely find a host of restaurants that are not part of the big chains. Example: a $25 coupon for dinner at an Italian restaurant at a cost of $4.

You can also choose from a multitude of other categories, including automotive, books & magazines, health care, office supplies, pet care, and professional services. For even more convenient saving, you can sign up to receive coupons by e-mail.

Coupon savings guru Stephanie Nelson has posted an e-book called *Drugstore Coupon Savings Strategies* on her website www. couponmom.com.

COUPONMOM.COM Clip coupons to your heart's content when you visit www.couponmom.com. You don't have to be a mom to take advantage of Stephanie Nelson's grocery and drugstore coupons. If you're looking for a coupon college, this is the place. Try the free videos, e-books, and tutorials. You'll also find lists of free samples for just about anything you can imagine. Follow another link to access coupon codes for big-name companies like Lands' End, JC Penney, and Amazon.com. Stephanie's blog lists even more sale prices and coupon deals at stores like Target, Walmart, and Walgreens.

You can also do well by doing good with Coupon Mom: The site encourages users to donate food items to charity (and explains how to do it in the FAQ section).

RESTAURANT.COM This is the go-to site for anyone who wants to have a nice but discounted meal out. Here's how it works: Go to www.restaurant.com and enter the zip code of the location you want. Once you decide on your dining spot, you can, for example, buy a $25 certificate for $10.

Caution: You might have to make a minimum purchase in order to use the certificate. For example, you may have to spend at least $50, so in the end the meal would cost you $25, not counting taxes and tips, on top of what you paid for the certificate, if you are using a $25 certificate.

Advantage: Unlike similar sites, you can purchase the discount the same day that you plan to use it. So you can make a last-minute decision. If you live in a city, you should be able to pick from lots of local, nonchain restaurants. Click the "special features" filter on the left of the page to find eateries that offer a senior discount or are wheelchair accessible. You can also order coupons by phone at 888-745-6991.

Access Restaurant.com and Coupons. com through the AARP website to get even better special deals. Members receive at least a 50 percent discount on restaurant gift certificates purchased at the Restaurant Discount Center. Special deals are also available through AARP's Grocery Coupon Center.

Spend a Little, Save a Lot

The last decade has seen the rise of a twist on an old business adage: You have to spend money to make money. The new idea is a little more counterintuitive: You have to spend money to *save* money. Paradoxical though it seems, it's the driving theory behind such coupon sites as Groupon and LivingSocial (which also add the pressure of a group mentality) and other sites—some of which you must pay a nominal fee to use.

Coupons for purchase

For devotees of the spending-to-save concept, these sites are gateways to serious savings. Here's how Groupon.com, one of the biggest "social shopping" sites, works:

IT'S A FACT!

Groupon makes its profit by keeping about half the money customers pay for their coupons.

Sign onto the site with your city and e-mail address, and you'll be taken to the deal of the day (you'll also begin receiving e-mails with the daily deals). Maybe it will be half price at a local restaurant or spa. When you spot a deal you like, buy it and enjoy.

There's one catch . . . at Groupon, a minimum number of people must sign up for every deal (not so at LivingSocial). Otherwise, no dice, and you should start watching for the next deal that will work for you. There is a sidebar on the site that shows whether the minimum number of people have bought the deal, how many have been bought total, how much time you have left to buy, and a summary of the deal (overall value, percentage off, and amount saved). So generally, you can be sure before you decide to sign up whether it will be worth your time—and money.

Here are some tips for using these sites:

■ Deals do sell out, so once you've decided to buy, don't hesitate too long.

■ If you're not sure whether to buy, check out the Groupon "Discussion" for reviews of products.

■ Stick with deals that are easy to get to. The biggest discount in the world won't work if you have to drive 200 miles to take advantage of it.

■ Deals have an expiration date, so make sure you know if you'll have enough time to use them.

> **IT'S A FACT!**
>
> What makes Groupon stand out from the crowd is its witty writing style. You'll want to read the description just for fun, even if you don't want the product. More than 400 writers are hard at work making it happen.

■ Read the fine print to make sure you're aware of all the conditions of the deal.

So, is this new shopping style a good choice for you? The experts say "maybe."

It's easy to get caught up in the energy of the online group that you can feel but can't see. Ask yourself: Am I really saving money on something I want or need? Or am I just caught up in the emotion of the moment? Is this product really cheaper than I could find it elsewhere? Do I really want this item? And once I've bought this coupon, what is the chance I just won't get around to using it?

If you do buy a voucher and then find you can't use it, you're not alone. About 10 to 20 percent of Groupon and LivingSocial coupons aren't redeemed. But you don't have to let your money go down the drain. Several websites have sprung up to help you recoup at least some of your money. Lifesta.com, CoupRecoup.com, and DealsGoRound.com all let you sell your Groupon and LivingSocial coupons.

Lifesta charges 99 cents and takes an 8 percent cut when you sell a coupon, and DealsGoRound charges 10 percent. CoupRecoup is free.

If you go to these coupon resale sites just to sell your unused vouchers, then you're missing some of the best deals in town. Search them to find and buy amazing deals for yourself or gifts too!

Oh, you shouldn't have—or should you?

Have you ever started looking for a gift for someone else and ended up buying yourself one as well? (Is the earth round?) Many people have learned that gift cards are an easy, small, portable way to give a present. They can be used to buy anything in the store (instead of coupons, which usually only apply to one type of item), make returns and exchanges unnecessary, and often don't expire—or at least they have a much longer "shelf life" than most coupons. They're the perfect gift.

But . . . there's more! Now gift cards are a great way to get a discount for yourself at the store of your choice. Of course it's nice if the gift card came from

One expert says that you might get the best discount by buying a gift card on eBay. When you do use the auction web site, make sure the seller feedback score is high—99 percent or better. Also, be sure to allow for the shipping cost.

someone else—but what if you get a $50 gift card for a store where you never shop? What a waste! Here's what you (or a tech-savvy buddy) can do: Sell the card for $40 online. You're happy because you have just gained $40, and your buyer is happy because she can get $50 worth of merchandise.

Where can this win-win transaction take place? To buy or sell a gift card, try eBay (search for "gift card") or www.giftcardgranny.com. Gift Card Granny pulls in sales from other gift card websites, so that makes it your go-to place. And you'll find an amazing list of discounts and freebies when you go to www.giftcardgranny.com/blog/senior-discounts. Example: at Golden Corral, get 10 percent off if you're over 60.

If you're watching for a certain store or stores, set up "alerts" at Gift Card Granny. You'll be notified by e-mail when the card you want is available.

The founder of Gift Card Granny, Luke Knowles, believes that someone who uses discounted gift cards on a regular basis can save up to $2,000 a year.

To be smart about gift cards, you have to plan ahead. If you buy online, figure about five days before the card is actually in your hands. Other tips when buying gift cards on the Internet:

■ The amount of discount you get will depend on how popular the store or retailer is. Don't expect a big discount if you buy a Target card, but do expect 10 percent or more off a restaurant card.

■ Watch for expiration dates, or a date after which the amount on the card may be charged a small fee for nonuse.

To be a successful gift-card shopper, you must be organized:

■ Keep all your cards in one place. Don't lose them.

■ Keep track of how much money is left on each card. Try placing a sticky note on the back of each card so you can write down the balance.

■ Toss the card when it's used up. It won't help to have an empty card taking up space in your wallet!

IT'S A FACT!

You can get your hands on gift cards in several ways, not just because someone gives you one as a present or you bought a discounted card on the Internet. They can also come from the stores themselves as part of a promotion. ("Buy this vacuum cleaner and get a $20 gift card as a bonus.")

The Silver-Haired Advantage

So far we've mostly covered coupons and discounts that are available to anyone with the pertinacity to find them. But what about all the discounts reserved for the older crowd? Let's explore some places where you'll be rewarded simply for being, well, on the "mature" side.

AARP: Helpful at Home

Anyone over 50 can pay $16 a year to be a member of AARP, the nonprofit association for people over age 50. Known for its senior advocacy, the group excels in corralling discounts for its members. Uncover the secret for everyday savings with your

AARP card. (Tip: To take advantage of the discounts, be sure to start from the AARP website.) Here are some examples:

HEALTHCARE For healthcare and medical expenses, you can access prescription discounts if you're not yet eligible for or not using Medicare Part D. If you have hearing loss, discounts include up to 20 percent off digital hearing aids. Vision discounts mean you can save at major eyewear retailers such as LensCrafters and JC Penney. You can also take advantage of monthly promotions at Walgreens, including their Health Essentials catalog.

FITNESS Are you a walker? Leslie Sansone's DVDs can keep you moving inside when the weather's acting up outside. Get 50 percent off her Walk Club membership and up to 50 percent off the DVDs with AARP. Find a trainer at the American Council of Exercise, then get 20 percent off all training sessions. You can also get discounts at Gold's Gym and for treadmills from Smooth Fitness.

Go to www.savings. com and put "senior citizen" in the search box. You'll pull up savings just for the boomer group.

SHOPPING & DINING What's more fun than that? When you're at a Tanger Shopping Center, stop in the mall's office to get a book with 20-percent-off discount offers. Then detour to Denny's on the way home. AARP members get 20 percent off the total check every day from 4–6 P.M. Coffee is $1 for AARP members and their guests every day, all day long.

CELL PHONES Want a cheap cell phone deal? Senior status can get you a break with several cell phone providers.

- Try Consumer Cellular. With plans starting at $10 per month, there are no contracts. AARP members save 5 percent on monthly service and usage charges and get a 30-percent discount on some accessories. You'll also get an expanded risk-free guarantee (45 days or 45 minutes instead of 30).

- AT&T offers the Special Senior Nation 200 Plan, which is only $29.99 per month if you're 65+.

- Jitterbug has $10 per month phone service if you're age 50 or older.

- Verizon's Nationwide 65 Plus Plan is just $29.99 per month if you're—you guessed it—65 or older.

EVERYDAY SAVINGS Your AARP member number logs you into the Everyday Savings Center. Look around, and you'll find discounts from more than 500 local and national retailers. An example: Get $7 off when you order $70 of merchandise from Target online. Other retailers include Home Depot, Omaha Steaks, JC Penney, Sears, and Kohl's. There

---

IT'S A FACT!

Four commonsense ways to really, really save money:

1. Be organized. Know what you need. If you're into coupons, have a system that keeps you on your toes.

2. Just because it's cheap doesn't mean you need it. Don't buy stuff you won't use or wouldn't ordinarily buy. If you do, you're wasting money.

3. Buy in bulk only if you know you'll use it. Have a place to store bargains if you have room, but don't turn into a hoarder.

4. If it looks like a bargain, it might not be. Comparison shop with your cell phone or online.

is a rewards program based on collecting points when you make purchases through Everyday Savings.

Entertainment

When it comes to leisure activities and entertainment, having senior status is the ticket to savings. Whether it's the opera or theater or movies or concerts, being a senior almost guarantees a break in ticket price. If you don't see a senior rate advertised, just ask. It's likely that you will receive one.

Audio books

Are you a reader who likes to enjoy books while you're walking around, cleaning the kitchen, or relaxing—with your eyes closed? Or maybe your eyes just aren't what they used to be. In other words, if you like audio books, you can download them for free on the Internet at www.librivox.org. You won't find the latest best seller, because they record only books that are no longer in copyright. But there are about 4,000 books to choose from, and with classics like *Oliver Twist* and *Ivanhoe* available, you should be able to find something to interest you.

> **IT'S A FACT!**
>
> Still have good eyes and want to help someone else enjoy literature? If you like to read out loud, you can volunteer to be a reader for LibriVox.

Going on a road trip? Audio books can help make the time—and the miles—fly by. But free computer downloads won't help you in the car, and audio books can be pricey. Enter Cracker Barrel!

The ubiquitous restaurant and store serving up good country food and atmosphere has created a perfect solution to expensive audio books. Simply buy a Books-On-Audio CD at whatever Cracker Barrel location you visit, listen to it (at home or on the road), and return it to any Cracker Barrel. They'll refund the purchase price, minus $3.49 per week that you've had it. It's that easy! Plus, you can get the best sellers not available on sites like LibriVox. And with Cracker Barrel restaurants located in much of the United States, you'll be sure to come across one sooner or later.

Movie time

Seniors almost always get movie theater discounts, but the amount of the discount and the age at which it kicks in varies.

REGAL CINEMAS This is the largest chain and discounts tickets up to 30 percent for people age 60 and over.

AMC The second-largest chain gives seniors 55 and over 30 percent off their tickets.

CINEMARK/CENTURY THEATERS This chain gives movie-goers age 62 and older 35 percent off. And on Mondays, they offer an additional 10 percent off all films (except 3D) at all show times.

One benefit of being retired is that you don't have to see a movie in the evening—when crowds are thick, theaters are full, and prices are high. Try a matinee or go on a weekday instead of a weekend; you'll pay less for your ticket and may score other discounts, too. For example, Regal Cinemas offers $2 candy on Mondays and $2 popcorn on Tuesdays—the only requirement is joining the Regal Crown Club (membership is free). As you use your card, you can build up points to use toward future discounts. Many theaters offer similar programs, though they're not always free (AMC's Stubs program costs $12 per year). Check with your theater for details.

Museums, aquariums, and zoos

Oh my! When was the last time you got up close and personal with an original Monet, watched a dolphin perform acrobatics, or laughed at an elephant dousing himself with water on a hot summer day? If it's been a while, maybe it's time for a visit to a local museum, aquarium, or zoo.

Many institutions offer senior discounts; amount and age requirement varies by location. Even better—some places have "free days" or "community days" when admission to the basic exhibits (not including special exhibits or shows) is free. Take advantage of those discounts, especially if free days are weekdays when there will be smaller crowds. Enjoy meandering through on your own or with a friend, or make it even more special and take the grandkids (children usually get discounted tickets too).

Groceries & Drugstores

As food prices increase, it can seem as if eating in is just as expensive as dining out. But it doesn't have to be—not if you take advantage of some of these discounts. Grocery stores vary considerably by region, but here are some more widespread stores and their age-friendly offers.

- Albertson's offers 10 percent off to people 55 and older the first Wednesday of the month.

- Great Valu Food Store and Harris Teeter will give you 5 percent off every Tuesday if you're 60 or older.

- Kroger offers 10 percent off, but applicable dates vary. Check your local store for details.

- Publix gives seniors 60 and older 5 percent off every Wednesday, but this offer is only valid outside of Florida.

Make sure you also take advantage of rewards programs, like Albertson's Preferred Card. These programs, which are often free to sign up for, allow you to take advantage of certain sales that are restricted to cardholders. Also check online for coupons and sales that may not be widely advertised in the newspaper sales fliers.

But who said you have to go to a grocery store for, well, groceries? If you shop drugstore chains like Walgreens, CVS, and Rite Aid, maybe you've picked up a box of gelatin, a can of coffee, or even a carton of ice cream from the freezer. If you make your drugstore a grocery destination, you can save big.

Ways to save: sales, coupons, store credit, rebates, and plain old coupons from the manufacturer. Start by checking the weekly insert (Sunday, maybe Wednesday). Or, as always, you can go online to see what's on sale for the week. Actually, if you order online, Walgreens will ship for free if your order is over $25 (and you'll save on the gas to take you there and back). CVS has a reward card that you can use instead of coupons. And Rite Aid will give

SENIOR SECRET

It's not quite winning the lottery, but almost. Watch for "Catalina" coupons at the grocery store or drugstore when you're checking out. They are printed out at the register. Many are just average coupons, but some are for money off ($1, $5 or even more) a shopping trip. What makes them great is that they can be spent on anything in the store. Shoppers miss out when they ignore the coupon. So be sure to check, every time. You might hit the jackpot.

you 10 percent off on Tuesdays, as well as 10 percent off prescriptions.

Convenient bonuses:

- You can get your prescriptions filled at the same time.
- Stores are small, so you can be in and out quickly.
- Drugstores are local and close to home.

Local Senior Discounts

At www.seniordiscounts.com, it says they're the "largest senior discount database anywhere" with 150,000 local businesses around the country. There's a catch, though: You can't dig into the database unless you buy the Gold Membership for $8 a year.

How about more discounts in your own neighborhood just for people over 55? A site introduced in early 2011 is Sciddy, where "seniors pay less." Sign in with your hometown or a travel destination where you want to look for a restaurant or B&B. You can search for discounts under major headings like travel, entertainment, health, and home services. For example, find a local dentist who will give you 10 percent off. Caution: Not every discount starts at the age-55 level. In some cases you might need to be 60 or 65. Find your nearby discounts at www.sciddy.com.

Stores love the kind of people who use coupons from the Internet. Online coupon users have higher incomes, shop more often, and spend more on groceries.

Restaurants

Lots of eateries offer discounts to older folks, no coupons or gift cards necessary. Discounts can vary by age requirement and day of the week, and sometimes they require a rewards-program membership.

In the box below you'll find a summary of some discounts at popular restaurant chains. But many others have similar programs—often all you have to do is ask. Policies and programs may change, so be sure to ask for details.

Restaurant	Discount	Age Req.
Applebee's	10% off (varies by location)	60+ (may vary)
Arby's	10%	55+
Burger King	10%	65+
Culver's	10%	60+
Denny's	20% for AARP members	55+
Dunkin' Donuts	10% off or free coffee	55+
IHOP	10%	55+
KFC	free small drink with meal purchase	55+
McDonald's	discount on coffee	55+
Sonic	10% off or free beverage	60+
Steak 'n Shake	10% off on Monday and Tuesday	50+ (may vary)
Subway	10%	60+
Waffle House	10% off on Monday	60+
Wendy's	10%	55+
White Castle	10%	62+

Shopping

For all you mall-walkers, many clothing and retail stores offer discounts as well. Here are some of the best discounts, whether you're shopping for yourself or your grandkids.

- Banana Republic offers a flat 10 percent off for people age 50 and older.

- Bon-Ton Department stores, which include Bergner's, Carson Pirie Scott, Elder-Beerman, and Younkers, among others, offer 15 percent off on senior discount days. You must be 55 or older to get this discount.

- Need some comfy shoes? Clarks will give you 10 percent off if you're 62 or older.

One of the best savings web sites is www.stretcher.com. That's for Dollar Stretcher.

- Dress Barn gives the 55+ crowd 10 percent off.

- If you're looking to stock up on birthday, holiday, and other greeting cards, stop by your nearest Hallmark store. You can get 10 percent off one day of the week; which day it is varies by location.

- Kohl's gives 15 percent off to those 60 and older.

- Prefer to shop more "thrift"-ily? Goodwill offers 10 percent off one day a week (check your local store to find out which day), and The Salvation Army Thrift Stores will give up to 50 percent off if you're 55 or older. You won't find a better deal than that!

Besides these discounts, many of these stores offer online coupons and allow you to sign up to receive special deals and offers via e-mail. If you regularly shop at a particular store, e-mail coupons may be a very convenient way to take advantage of as many discounts as possible.

Travel

You spent your working years saving for retirement so you could spend some well-deserved time relaxing and letting someone else do the work—often, away from home. Seniors love to take trips, and travel companies know it. They want seniors as customers, and there are plenty of deals to be had. Here are some to get you started.

PLANES Cheap—or at least more affordable—airfares. Take off with these tips:

- For a round-trip, be ready to buy one-way tickets on two different airlines.
- Check to see if it is cost-effective to fly in and out of different airports.

IT'S A FACT!

The days of special air fares for seniors are long gone...with some exceptions. Check out Southwest Airlines, which offers discounts for travelers age 65 and older, at its website www.southwest.com, or call customer service at 800-435-9792. A great benefit: Senior fares are fully refundable if you need to cancel. You can find an occasional senior bargain on other major airlines, but you'll have to dig around their websites, and you might find better rates by other methods.

- Tuesday, Wednesday, and Saturday are the best travel days of the week; save 5–25 percent.
- If you'll need a hotel or car rental at your destination, package deals can make the whole trip less expensive.
- Sign up for the airlines' last-minute fare lists. They release bargain seats when they're not sold out. Or get on the e-mail list for www.airfarewatchdog.com; they'll send you fare alerts.

Some airlines offer discounts for seniors, though you'll have to call to be sure. Here are a few possibilities:

- Alaska Airlines offers 10 percent off for those 65 and older.
- American Airlines, United Airlines, and U.S. Airways will sometimes give discounts for people 65 and older; call for details.
- Southwest Airlines offers senior discounts to travelers age 65 and older. Call customer service for details. A bonus of flying Southwest? No baggage fees!

TRAINS Unlike the airlines, Amtrak offers a clear senior discount. You must be 62 years old to receive a 15 percent discount on the lowest fare for most Amtrak trains. Going to Canada? If you're 60, you can get 10 percent off a cross-border fare between Amtrak and VIA Rail Canada.

BUS For cheap bus travel in the United States, Canada, and Great Britain, try Megabus. In the United States, Megabus operates in the northeast part of the country, from Iowa and Missouri on the west to Tennessee and North Carolina in the south. There are no special rates for seniors, but reserve early and you might snag their famous $1 fare. There's always a 50-cent reservation fee and another half dollar to change reservations. Take a look at www.megabus.com.

Greyhound and Peter Pan bus lines offer a 5-percent senior discount for seniors 62 and over. If you're 65, you can get 10 percent off some parts of the Trailways schedule.

CAR RENTAL So you found your discounted airfare or train or bus ticket, and now you've arrived at your trip destination. Need a rental car? You can get some good deals on that, too.

If you're an AARP member, you can get up to 25 percent off on rentals with Alamo, Avis, and Hertz. Budget will

SENIOR SECRET

Even if you don't travel a lot, pick one hotel/motel travel reward program and stick with it. That way you'll build up points faster and get a "freebie" night or two more quickly. When you're deciding on the hotel chain that works best for you, look at the points per dollar and how quickly that can add up to a free overnight. Are the lodgings located where you usually travel or intend to travel? Are they combined with other companies that you like to use? (Several are affiliated with Amtrak.) And…can you get a good senior discount too?

Rated "best travel reward program," Marriott includes more than 3,000 lodgings, ranging from the high-end luxury Ritz Carlton to the lower cost Courtyard and Fairfield Inns. The standard senior discount is 15 percent off standard rates. You must be 62, don't have to belong to AARP or AAA, and you can reserve two rooms at the senior rate, so bring the grandkids.

Other highly rated reward programs: Hilton HHonors program, Wyndham Rewards, InterContinental Priority Club, Hyatt Gold Passport, Choice Privileges, Best Western Rewards, and Starwood Preferred Guest.

give you 20 percent off (10 percent without AARP membership), Enterprise will give you 5 percent off, and National Rent-A-Car will give up to 30 percent off.

■ Dollar Rent-A-Car offers seniors age 50 and over 10 percent off, no AARP membership necessary.

HOTELS There's no question that a hotel can make or break a vacation—in terms of both comfort and cost. To ensure peace of mind for you and your wallet, check out some of these senior deals.

■ Hotel operator Choice Hotels offers people 60 and over 20–30 percent off. This is a great deal, especially when you consider the range of hotel options covered by Choice Hotels: Clarion, Comfort Inn, Comfort Suites, EconoLodge, Mainstay Suites, Quality Inn, Rodeway Inn, and Sleep Inn (plus a few others).

■ Other hotels offer discounts, as well: Get 10 percent off at Hampton Inns & Suites when you book 72 hours in advance; Holiday Inn offers 10–30 percent off for people 62 and over, depending on location; Hyatt Hotels will give you 25–50 percent off if you're 62 and over; Marriott gives seniors 62 and up 15 percent off; and the InterContinental Hotels Group gives various discounts if you're 65+. Call for details and to confirm prices.

AARP: On Board for Travel Discounts

AARP's benefits are many and varied, especially when it comes to travel. And if plan your trip through the Expedia–AARP website, you'll be rewarded with savings on top of AARP's other travel deals. Example: You'll get another 10 percent off participating hotel rates and up to $100 credit to spend onboard some cruises.

TOURS Special interest tours with discounts include:

■ DuVine Adventures bicycle tours in North America, South America, and Europe: AARP members get $75 off per person and free champagne.

■ Road Scholar (formerly Elderhostel) offers a free gift for AARP members on some tours. See more about Road Scholar in Chapter 7.

■ Journeys Unlimited, a tour company that serves the Christian community, gives AARP members $50 or $100 off their trips, depending on tour cost.

■ For Catholics, Regina Tours offers spiritual journeys and pilgrimages with savings of $50 or $100, depending on tour cost.

■ With Untours, all your travel arrangements are made but you have freedom to explore. Get a $75 discount per person.

SENIORS LOVE CRUISES And it appears AARP loves cruises, too.

■ MSC Cruises includes a $50 per person discount for booking early and other extras.

■ Hurtigruten/Norwegian Coastal features a $35 per person onboard credit on select cruises to Antarctica, the Arctic, and Greenland.

■ Norwegian Cruise Line offers a 5-percent discount on travels to the Caribbean and Bahamas, Europe, and New England. Catch: You must book at least nine months in advance.

■ Variety Cruises offers a $75 discount per person on its Mediterranean small ship cruises. Destinations include Greece, Turkey, the Red Sea, and the Adriatic Sea.

■ Blount Small Ship Adventures specializes in cruising where larger ships can't go. Plus, receive up to $100 shipboard credit. Trips include locations in the United States, Canada, and the Caribbean.

Classic tours to Europe and around the globe are offered by Collette Vacations and Grand European Tours. General Tours Small Group Traveler has a limit of 16 guests on its tours. All are AARP-approved vendors and offer a range of discounts for AARP members.

Just to make sure you are getting a rock-bottom hotel room price, call the hotel itself (not its national 800 number) and ask them to beat your best Internet price.

HOTELS Discounts are widely available through AARP. Start at the AARP website to search for lodging. That way you'll be eligible for the best prices. When reserving or registering, you may need to give a member discount number.

Here is a selection of hotel companies and their discounts.

■ Choice Hotels: Discount is 10 percent off. Lodgings include the hotels on page 143—from basics like Sleep Inn and EconoLodge up to Comfort Suites and Cambria Suites. It also includes the more upscale and unique "Ascend" hotels. Choice also offers a reward program and special deals on its AARP website.

■ Starwood Hotels: Save 20 percent at one of the 975 worldwide hotels in this chain. Brands include Element, Four Points by Sheraton, Westin, and the luxurious LeMeridien.

- Wyndham Hotels: Get up to 20 percent off the best available rate. Wyndham operates these hotels: Wyndham Hotels and Resorts, Ramada, Days Inn, Super 8, Wingate, Baymont Inn & Suites, Microtel Inns & Suites, Hawthorn Suites, Howard Johnson, Travelodge, and Knights Inn.

- Best Western: Save 10 percent on more than 2,000 motels in the United States (4,000 globally). Besides the discounts, many Best Westerns offer extras such as complimentary upgrades or continental breakfast.

- La Quinta: Save 10 percent at the more than 800 hotels in North America. There's a rewards program based on points per dollar spent at La Quinta Inns and Suites hotels.

IT'S A FACT!

Sure, you're a member of AARP and are familiar with their deals on travel and other things. But have you joined AAA?

AAA is a motor club and travel company that provides, among other things, roadside assistance in case of a breakdown; a helpful travel agency and informational materials including guidebooks, maps, and access to travel odds and ends such as International Driving Permits; insurance (including Auto, Home, and Life); and special rates with restaurants, shops, hotels, car rental companies, and more. Membership cost varies depending on which type you choose, but here's the best part—seniors get a discount! That's right: You can get a discount for a membership that will get you even more discounts, and may even save your life in a roadside emergency. For more information and to look at a member handbook (where many, many discounts are listed), visit www.aaa.com.

- Hyatt Hotels: Get 10 percent off the daily rate at Hyatt Hotels & Resorts, Hyatt Place, or Summerfield Suites. In addition, the third night is either free or 50 percent off the daily rate.

- Hampton Inn: Save 10 percent off its best rate, subject to availability. Like many lodgings, it includes a free hot breakfast.

Miscellaneous

Here are a few more places where your senior status can help you out:

- Bally Total Fitness: If you're 62 or older, you can get up to $100 off a membership.

- Your hair may be thinner than it used to be, but that doesn't mean it couldn't use a trim! For customers who are 60+, Great Clips offers $3 off haircuts, and Super Cuts will take $2 off.

TOP SECRET ★ TOP SECRET ★ SENIOR SECRET ★ TOP SECRET ★ TOP SECRET

Like free stuff? Who doesn't? Here are two places to find some: www.freecycle.com and www.craigslist.com. These are virtual shopping malls where people are willing to give away good stuff they just can't use anymore. On the other side of the coin, if you're clearing out and decluttering, these sites are a great way to find a new home for your unwanted (but still usable) stuff. Takers are expected to pick up their new possessions, so there's no driving for you. For safety's sake, have someone at home with you at pickup time or, if you have a garage with a remote opener, put the item in the garage so you can open the garage door from inside.

Senior Resources

DATING & ROMANCE

Looking for Mr. or Ms. Right? The following are matchmaking services that seniors like:

eHarmony.com

www.eharmony.com
800-951-2023

Match.com

www.match.com

Seniors.com

www.seniors.com

DIET AND FITNESS

The American Dietetic Association
This site includes a wealth of information about eating right, including a special section for seniors.

www.eatright.org
American Dietetic Association
120 South Riverside Plaza,
Suite 2000
Chicago, IL 60606-6995
800-877-1600

USDA Dietary Guidelines

This government site explains how to follow a healthful diet.

www.dietaryguidelines.gov
Center for Nutrition Policy
   and Promotion
3101 Park Center Drive
10th Floor
Alexandria, VA 22302-1594
703-305-7600

EMPLOYMENT

Experience Works

This is a national, community-based group that helps older adults get the training they need to find good jobs in their communities. It's for people age 55 and older who are unemployed.

www.experienceworks.org
Experience Works, Inc.
4401 Wilson Boulevard
Suite 1100
Arlington, VA 22203
866-EXP-WRKS (397-9757)

Seniors4Hire

This is a nationwide online career center that claims to be the number-one place on the Internet for businesses that value a diverse workforce. They actively recruit folks in the United States age 50 and older, including retirees and senior citizens.

www.seniors4hire.org
The Forward Group
OBO Seniors4Hire.org
7071 Warner Avenue F466
Huntington Beach, CA 92647
714-840-0200

SeniorJobBank

SeniorJobBank helps employers and qualified older job seekers find each other.

www.seniorjobbank.org
NHC Group, Inc.
PO Box 508
Marlborough, MA 01752
888-501-0804

Workforce 50

A sister site of SeniorJobBank, Workforce 50 helps mature job seekers find meaningful employment opportunities. In addition to job postings, it offers articles on a variety of job-related topics written by experts.

www.workforce50.com
NHC Group, Inc.
PO Box 508
Marlborough, MA 01752
E-mail: info@jobmark.com

FAMILY

Grandparents As Parents

If you are one of the millions of seniors who is parenting a grandchild, you'll find resources here that can help.

www.grandparentsasparents
  .org
Grandparents As Parents
22048 Sherman Way
Suite 217
Canoga Park, CA 91303
818-264-0880

Grandparents.com

This site gives you practical tips and offers thoughtful articles about your role in the family.

www.grandparents.com
589 8th Avenue, 6th Floor
New York, NY 10018
646-839-8800

FAMILY HISTORY

Ancestry.com

This site claims to be the world's largest online family history resource.

www.ancestry.com
360 West 4800 North
Provo, UT 84604
800-ANCESTRY

Archives.com

This site has millions of documents online for you to search. You get a seven-day free trial. Contact for customer support only.

www.genhomepage.com
Archives Headquarters
101 University Avenue

Suite 320
Palo Alto, CA 94307

Ellis Island

If your ancestors came to America by way of Ellis Island, it's free to search for the name of their ship.

www.ellisisland.org
The Statue of Liberty–Ellis Island Foundation, Inc.
Attention: History Center
17 Battery Place #210
New York, NY 10004-3507
212-561-4588

The National Genealogical Society

The society will teach you how to research your family history through tutorials and articles on its website. Some aspects of the site are limited to members, who pay a fee to join.

www.ngsgenealogy.org
3108 Columbia Pike
Suite 300
Arlington, VA 22204
703-525-0050

FOR SENIORS ONLY

AARP

If you go to just one website for senior-related material, visit AARP. For more than 50 years, it has specialized in and advocated for people who are age 50 and older. AARP knows the territory and covers every topic related to senior life.

www.aarp.org
AARP
601 E Street NW
Washington, D.C. 20049
888-687-2277

AARP Internet Resources

This is AARP's database of more than 1,200 of the best Internet sites for people age 50 and older. You can search by topic and category.

www.aarp.org/internetresources

About.com Senior Living

Senior-specific topics are covered here, including articles such as "Travel can help you live longer" and "The 4 best exercises for older adults."

http://seniorliving.about.com

Go60.com

This site focuses on news and the positive aspects of getting older.

www.go60.com
3087 W. Wilbur Avenue
Coeur d'Alene, ID 83815
E-mail: contact@go60.com

Gray Panthers

Gray Panthers is an activist group supporting senior issues as well as social and economic justice and peace.

www.graypanthers.org
1612 K Street NW
Suite 300
Washington, D.C. 20006
800-280-5362 or 202-737-6637

ITNAmerica

ITN stands for "Independent Transportation Network." The site is a portal to dignified transportation for seniors, who can trade their own cars for rides from volunteers.

www.itnamerica.com
90 Bridge Street
Suite 100
Westbrook, ME 04092
207-857-9001

Wired Seniors

This site covers topics of interest to seniors, using the Internet as a way to connect.

www.wiredseniors.com
Contact by e-mail through the form on the website.

GOVERNMENT

BenefitsCheckup.org

A service of the National Council on Aging, this helps those age 55 and older with limited income and resources to find public and private benefits for which they are eligible but are not receiving.

www.benefitscheckup.org
For more information, contact them at comments@benefitscheckup.org

Catalog of Federal Domestic Assistance

This site lets you look for all federal programs that provide resources to state and local governments.

www.cfda.gov
Contact customer service at 866-606-8220.

The Centers for Medicare and Medicaid Services (CMS)

This site is a compendium of all the health programs managed by the federal government. You can browse by topic, by agency, and by provider type. The site also has numerous tools and resources.

http://cms.hhs.gov
7500 Security Boulevard
Baltimore, MD 21244

Eldercare.gov

A service of the U.S. Administration on Aging, this site has an eldercare locator that allows you to search by topic or by zip code for everything from Alzheimer's to volunteerism.

www.eldercare.gov
800-677-1116

Medicare

Medicare is the federal government's program that provides health care coverage for seniors.

www.medicare.gov
Centers for Medicare & Medicaid Services
7500 Security Boulevard
Baltimore, MD 21244
800-633-4227

National Conference of State Social Security Administrators

These are the Social Security administrators for each state. To find the SSA for your state, click "About" and then "State Administrators" in the menu on the left side of the page.

www.ncsssa.org

National Council on Aging

This government agency is a good place to start as you look for government services for seniors.

www.ncoa.org
1901 L Street NW, 4th Floor
Washington, D.C. 20036
202-479-1200

National Institutes of Health

NIH is the nation's research agency. The Health Information section offers information on just about any health issue, as well as on clinical trials.

www.nih.gov
National Institutes of Health
9000 Rockville Pike
Bethesda, MD 20892
301-496-4000

Social Security Administration

The official website of the Social Security Administration answers your questions.

www.socialsecurity.gov
Social Security Administration
Office of Public Inquiries
Windsor Park Building
6401 Security Boulevard
Baltimore, MD 21235
800-772-1213
7 A.M.–7 P.M. EST (Mon.–Fri.)

USA.gov

Enter "seniors" in the search box to open the door to just about every area of government information and advice you can imagine.

www.usa.gov
800-FED-INFO (800-333-4636)
8 A.M.–8 P.M. EST (Mon.–Fri.)—
except federal holidays

HEALTH

Active and Able

If you are looking for a little help getting around and getting things done, you can find the tools you're looking for here. You can shop by room (for instance "bathroom") or by category (such as "alarms and alerts").

www.activeandable.com
2173 Oxford Road
Des Plaines, IL 60018
877-229-9993
8 A.M.–6 P.M. CST

Alliance for Aging Research

Focuses on medical research to improve the health of older people. The resources section is comprehensive and includes links to statistics, caregiving, clinical trials, diseases and conditions, general health, health and aging agencies and institutes, health insurance, health news, legal resources, magazines and journals, medication safety, minority health, and patient care.

www.agingresearch.org
750 17th St. NW
Suite 1100
Washington, D.C. 20006
202-293-2856

DocFinder

Check the license status of a doctor that you'd like to know more about. This site is sponsored by Administrators in Medicine, executives who lead medical and osteopathic boards for each state.

*www.docboard.org/docfinder
.html*

Hospital Compare

This site lets you compare all the hospitals in your area according to general information, quality of care, and Medicare payment. It also provides contact information if you have a complaint about your hospital experience.

www.hospitalcompare.hhs.gov
U.S. Department of Health
    and Human Services
200 Independence Avenue SW
Washington, D.C. 20201
877-696-6775

Kaiser Health News

This nonprofit news organization is committed to in-depth coverage of health care policy and politics. You can follow the news about health care–related issues on its website.

www.kaiserhealthnews.org
Kaiser Family Foundation
  Headquarters
2400 Sand Hill Road
Menlo Park, CA 94025

Contact by e-mail through the form on the website.

Mayo Clinic

The world-famous Mayo Clinic offers a wealth of medical information on diseases and conditions, symptoms, drugs and supplements, tests and procedures, a healthy lifestyle, and first aid. Its guides to medical conditions provide a section about preparing for your doctor appointment, including a list of questions to ask. Contact is by e-mail through the website.

www.mayoclinic.com

Medicare Interactive

This is not a government site, but it offers extensive information on Medicare and its specifics, as well as rights, protections, advice, and resources for caregivers.

www.medicareinteractive.org

My Family History

This site is a tool created by the U.S. Surgeon General for you to record and track your family health history. It can be shared with your health care providers, who will use it to assess your risk for some diseases.

http://familyhistory.hhs.gov
E-mail: fhh@hhs.gov
888-478-4423

Quack Watch

This is the most complete resource on health frauds. You'll also find links to health-related information, including tips for provider selection, health promotion, and disease management.

www.quackwatch.org
Chatham Crossing
Suite 107/208
11312 U.S. 15-501 North
Chapel Hill, NC 27517
919-533-6009

U.S. Pharmacoepeia

The USP is a nongovernmental, nonprofit public standard-setting authority for prescription and over-the-counter medications and other health-related products made or sold in the United

States. Its voluntary testing and auditing program verifies the quality, purity, and potency of dietary supplements. If you decide to take supplements or herbs that are not regulated by the Food and Drug Administration, check them at this site.

www.uspverified.org
12601 Twinbrook Parkway
Rockville, MD 20852-1790
800-227-8772

WebMD

This is a highly respected medical site that provides medical information covering a huge range of health conditions. Your doctor might have the WebMD magazine in the waiting room.

www.webmd.com

Contact by e-mail through the form on the website.

Your Guide to Medicare's Preventive Services

This booklet tells you about wellness provisions from the Affordable Care Act of 2010. Type www.medicare.gov/ publications/pubs/pdf/10110 .pdf into your browser's search box.

LEGAL

NOLO Law for All

This site will help you research a legal issue. It provides information in straightforward language, not legalese. Nolo also publishes books and includes a directory of lawyers by specialty and location.

www.nolo.com
Nolo Customer Sales & Service
950 Parker St.
Berkeley, CA 94710
800-728-3555

LEISURE AND VOLUNTEERING

Connected Living

Learn computer skills so you can stay connected with family, friends, and the community by using current technology.

www.connectedliving.com
Connected Living
300 Congress Street
Quincy, MA 02169
800-223-5080

National Senior Service Corps, Helping Seniors Help America

This program opens the door for seniors over age 55 to use their life experience to help others.

www.seniorcorps.org

Oasis—discover life after 50

This is a national network of education centers and community partners that promotes successful aging through lifelong learning, health programs, and volunteer engagement.

www.oasisnet.org
Oasis Institute
7710 Carondelet
Suite 125
St. Louis, MO 63105
314-862-2933

United We Serve

A nationwide service initiative to help meet the growing social needs as a result of the economic downturn. This is the best online resource for finding volunteer opportunities in your community and also for creating your own.

www.serve.gov
Corporation for National and
    Community Service
1201 New York Avenue, NW
Washington, D.C. 20525
202-606-5000

Volunteer.gov

This is America's natural and cultural resources volunteer portal. You can search for volunteer opportunities by keyword, location, type of work, and agency.

www.volunteer.gov/gov
Contact info is available for each agency.

PERSONAL FINANCE/ MONEY MANAGEMENT

Bankrate.com

This is a trusted site with a breadth of information that can't be beat. It covers the full range of financial information, including retirement.

www.bankrate.com

Charles Schwab

Schwab pioneered discount brokerage when fees were deregulated in the 1970s. The firm offers low-cost trading and investment information.

www.schwab.com
866-232-9890

Fidelity Investments

This is one of the largest mutual fund and financial advisory and management companies in the United States. It's also a discount brokerage firm.

www.fidelity.com
800-343-3548

Financial Industry Regulatory Authority

FINRA is the largest independent regulator for all securities firms that do business in the United States. It provides a wealth of information on protecting yourself and smart investing, as well as market data.

www.finra.org
FINRA
1735 K Street
Washington, D.C. 20006
301-590-6500

FindABetterBank

Pop in your zip code to find a bank with better rates or checking fees.

www.findabetterbank.com
Facilitas, Inc.
247 West 37th Street
New York, NY 10018
212-738-9292

Investopedia

If you want to find out more about a type of investing or wonder what an investment-related term means, this site can help.

www.investopedia.com

Morningstar

This firm provides perhaps the widest array of investment information and ratings. Basic membership is free, and there is expanded access for a fee. You'll also find calculators for

everything from savings to IRAs, data reports, and financial strategy lessons.

www.morningstar.com
Global Headquarters
22 West Washington Street
Chicago, IL 60602
312-696-6000

Securities and Exchange Commission (SEC)

This is the government agency whose mission is to protect investors, maintain fair and efficient markets, and facilitate capital formation. Contact by e-mail through the form on the website.

www.sec.gov
SEC Headquarters
100 F Street, NE
Washington, D.C. 20549
888-SEC-6585

Vanguard

Founder John Bogle created the idea of index funds when he was in college. Vanguard offers a wide range of index funds and serves as a full-service investment advisor.

www.vanguard.com
Vanguard
PO Box 2600
Valley Forge, PA 19482
877-662-7447

SAVING MONEY

All Things Frugal

It's the home of The Penny Pincher and Tightwad Tidbits ezines. Enough said.

www.allthingsfrugal.com

CouponMom.com

One of the best, especially for grocery and drugstore items. Includes ideas for being a more savvy coupon clipper.

www.couponmom.com
E-mail from the website.

Coupons.com

This huge coupon resource includes local restaurants that are not part of the big chains.

www.coupons.com
Coupons.com Inc.
400 Logue Avenue
Mountain View, CA 94043
650-605-4600

Dollar Stretcher.com

There's no special section for seniors, but Dollar Stretcher is one of the most complete savings websites. Type "seniors" into the search box (make sure that the Stretcher circle is checked, not Google) for senior-oriented articles.

www.stretcher.com
Dollar Stretcher

PO Box 14160
Bradenton, FL 34280
941-761-7805

Frugal Village

Simple living, cooking, family, and more are covered here. Get ideas for seniors by typing "senior citizen" in the search box.

www.frugalvillage.com
Sara Noel
c/o United Uclick
130 Walnut St.
Kansas City, MO 64106

Gift Card Granny

This site functions as a marketplace that connects people who want to sell an unused gift card with buyers who pay for it at a discounted price.

www.giftcardgranny.com
E-mail info@giftcardgranny
   .com

Lifesta

If you have bought a savings voucher from Groupon or LivingSocial and then can't use it, you can sell it on Lifesta.

www.lifesta.com
E-mail: support@lifesta.com
347-286-8431

Sciddy

Started in 2011, Sciddy is a resource for people age 50

and older to find discounts on all kinds of products and services right in their own city.

www.sciddy.com
888-257-4115
E-mail using the form on the website.

Senior Discounts

This site specializes in savings for people age 50 and older.

www.seniordiscounts.com
SeniorDiscounts.com
4811-A Hardware Drive NE
Suite 4
Albuquerque, NM 87109
505-366-1663

SENIOR FOCUS

National Committee to Preserve Social Security & Medicare

National Committee to Preserve Social Security & Medicare is against cuts in these two government programs. Membership costs $12 and up.

http://ncpssm.org
10 G Street NE
Suite 600
Washington, D.C. 20002
800-966-1935

Senior Journal

Find news and information just for seniors on this website.

www.seniorjournal.com

Suddenly Senior

A collection of news and information with a senior slant. Search for the list of Top 100 Senior & Boomer Blogs & Websites.

www.suddenly senior.com

ThirdAge

For senior women, this website includes recent news headlines, health issues, tips for aging well, beauty, and style for "living life to its fullest."

www.thirdage.com

SMART SHOPPING

Consumer Action

This is a gateway to becoming a smarter consumer. At the Consumer Action website, you can download the Consumer Action handbook.

www.consumeraction.gov
Federal Citizen Information Center
U.S. General Services Administration
1275 First Street NE, 11th Floor
Washington, D.C. 20417
202-501-1794

Gas Buddy

Find the cheapest gas in your neighborhood.

www.gasbuddy.com
7964 Brooklyn Boulevard #318
Brooklyn Park, MN 55445

TRAVEL

Frommers

Since Arthur Frommer shook up tourism with *Europe on $5 a Day* in the 1960s, he's still helping travelers get the most for their money. Check the section for seniors under "trip ideas."

www.frommers.com

Seniors Home Exchange

This cost-saving approach to vacationing and travel helps you arrange to switch homes with another senior. You may also arrange to visit with them in their home and then return the courtesy to them.

www.seniorshomeexchange .com
To contact via e-mail, click "contact wired seniors" at the bottom of the home page.

National Park Service

This site is the gateway to U.S. national parks. Seniors can get a lifetime pass for $10.

www.nps.gov

URBAN LEGEND DETECTOR

Snopes.com

In this day and age, it's hard to separate fact from rumor. But this site provides impeccable research to dispute or back up all those stories and rumors you hear about or read, especially on the Internet. Also makes for fascinating reading.

www.snopes.com
Contact via comments submission from the website.